ABCs OF HEALING FEELINGS

# THE
# KELLEY

## ABCs OF HEALING FEELINGS
### (A Neurocognitive Affective Positive Ego Building System)

RONALD L. KELLEY, MD, DLFAPA

ISBN 978-1-64468-499-3 (Paperback)
ISBN 978-1-64468-500-6 (Digital)

Covenant Books, Inc.
11661 Hwy 707
Murrells Inlet, SC 29576
www.covenantbooks.com

*"Mind forged manacles"* beat all the prisons man can make.
—William Blake/Ronald Kelley
(1757–1827; 1939–____)

# FOREWORD

As children, one of our first major feats is to master recitation of the alphabet. Each solitary letter strung along in a cherished singsong soon takes on new meaning. With these letters, we create words, and a new world is open to us. It becomes a world in which we have the power to reconstruct our emotions, illuminate our being, and record memories, a world in which we have the power to manage our ideas and ultimately for some who are gifted to ponder the meaning of life and the existence of the universe.

We begin to have the experiences that shape us into the person we are today.

*Becoming the person we want to be requires the deliberate self-manipulation (creative use) of tools of emotion, thought, reflection and mindfulness.*

Some days we glide along with ease on the waters of life with mirrored symmetry. Other days we are tossed about like a stone on an unforgiving seashore. How do we emerge from such turbulence with a calm core and polished exterior?

The *ABCs of Healing Feelings* is built on a framework of self-acceptance. Each *alphabetic prompt* promotes a collection of positive feelings based on memory and introspection. Memorizing and mastering the meanings of each letter through personal association opens a world of self-healing. Practice of the *ABCs of Healing Feelings* helps to self-soothe in times of distress. The letters and their definitions become a rolodex of an encouraging and uplifting system stored within the self, available to flip through at any time.

Internally recite your alphabet anywhere—sitting anxiously in a doctor's office, waiting in line at a bustling supermarket, stuck in snail's pace traffic, or resting your head on your pillow at the end of a long day. You may be surprised at the alphabet rhythm that occurs before long, and the joy and amusement, which stems from your own unique "song."[1]

You are on the path to awakening the innate ability to gracefully rise above a negative altercation, escape the lockdown of a dark memory, or hush the negative self-perceptions that hinder productivity and opportunity.

It's as easy as learning your ABCs.[2]

Sam Kelley, M.D.
Fellowship in Child Psychiatry
McLean Hospital
Harvard Medical School
Boston, MA

# PREFACE

Perhaps we became human when we developed the mentation[3] to make tools,[4] which are now uncountable. I invite you to realize that mental processes of ideas (cognitions), images (imaginations), and emotions (affects), are mental tools[5] that belong to and are used by the perceptions of our consciousness. Consciousness is a mysterious everyday miracle as we awaken to it throughout our lives.[6][7] Perception as a working definition for our purposes is the point of our awareness of external objects (other living life and things) and internal objects (ideas, sensations, images, and feelings).[8][9][10][11]

We learn numerous mental tools from our family, culture, and education system but less so the invaluable tools to manage our collection of images, ideas, and emotions[12][13] relevant to our relationship between the, I and the, me (our self-reflected thoughts, images, and feelings).

This ego building technique teaches and coaches you systematically how to use a variety of positive mental tools to self-develop greater ego strengths in your pursuit of happiness.[14] The greater the number of tools a carpenter has, the greater his or her ability to build a house. The more mental tools one has, the more one can rebuild one's own house of thought, ideas, feelings, and actions for greater happiness and adaptability.

Choice is another mystery of consciousness.[15] We all know the debate over whether we have free choice or are our choices determined by the indoctrination by our families, friends, culture, education, and our complicated biological system. It may be that both are truths. We can be compared to the trainer and rider of a horse who must train the horse according to the nature of the horse, just as the trainer of a dog must train according to the nature of the dog. We must train our biological system according to its nature.[16]

Our choice may be to become the rider of our nature and our mental tools become the saddle, bit, and harnesses to direct our deliberate conscious choices.

*"The greatest discovery of my generation is the fact that one can alter one's life by the altering of one's attitude."*
*(William James, 1842–1910)*

These tools which I have accumulated and developed with many patients for more than thirty years have helped many patients to not only overcome many of their mental maladies but to enhance their lives, relationships, jobs, spirituality, and joy of living.

In the last two decades, there has been a renaissance of psychological interest in positive psychology. I encourage you to read the research of Drs. Martin Seligman[17] and Barbara Frederickson[18] on positive psychology.

# INTRODUCTION

*The Kelley ABCs of Healing Feelings* is an ego building technique that is to be practiced repeatedly in intervals of time until the positive feelings[19] [20] [21] are present most of the time. Eventually, the entire technique can be exercised in a few minutes. It is advised that you diligently practice the ABCs in intervals of five (5) to fifteen (15) minutes, six (6) to twelve (12) times a day, thirty (30) to sixty (60) minutes apart for each practice until the positive healing feelings (HF) become automatic in the unconscious mind. This usually takes three (3) to six (6) months. Later, the technique can be used with a variety of personal crises, self-healing problems as well as personal self-development and/or fulfillment of one's aspirations.

Alternate methods will also work, such as practicing one or more healing feeling for one (1) to fifteen (15) minutes waiting a minimum of ten (10) minutes, then repracticing the same one or more healing feelings for one (1) to fifteen (15) minutes waiting a second time for a minimum of ten (10) minutes and repracticing a third time one or more of the same healing feelings for one (1) to fifteen (15) minutes. This is a neuroscientific proven long-term memory enhancement technique. This "spaced learning" technique can be practiced intermittently during one day and doing the same and/ or a different one or more the next day. It is important to individualize this method due to individual learning styles.[22] [23] [24] [25] *Healing feelings* in this instruction do not include the negative pleasure many feel in vengeance, sadism, or negative criticism.[26] [27] [28] [29]

The *ABCs of Healing Feelings* technique is based on a "peg" memory system.[30] [31] The letters of the English alphabet are consecutive pegs and permanent memories in the English speaker. Each letter thus becomes in this *ego building technique a healing letter. A healing word* (HW) is linked to the peg letter (healing letter) of the alphabet by the first letter of the *healing word.*

For example, the first letter of the alphabet is "A," and the *healing word* choice may be *acceptance.*[32][33][34]

The second link is the positive healing concept such as learning to remember a memory of the feeling of *acceptance* for one's self, others, pets, or by others or pets.

The third link is the healing concept used with a bridge of feeling.[35]

This *bridge of feeling* is a mental process where one does an inner memory search for any recollection of when the specified positive feeling had ever been felt in the near or distant past. When the selected positive feeling is remembered and felt in the past sense of experience, it is also immediately and automatically bridged from the past to the immediate present sense of time. The *bridge of feeling* or if the following terminology is preferred, a transfer of the healing feelings is the third link in the healing feeling technique. The experience of any *healing feeling* is an immediate pleasurable experience and serves as an internal self-reward. Eventually the *healing feeling* will serve as a part of an internal nucleus of unifying positive feelings.[36] This process is an internal operant conditioning of one's nervous system to be happy most of the time. It develops habit formation[37][38] among positive mood centers in the human brain[39] by stimulating the increased branching of nerve connections, increasing the making of pleasure nerve chemicals and brain nerve systems that have more control over negative mood centers in the brain.[40][41][42]

Follow the initial and basic process below:

The first example is as follows:

# A

"A" is a healing letter for a healing word that begins with the letter A.

*Acceptance* is initially recommended as a healing concept.[43][44] In this example, it is the concept of *acceptance* for one's self, "myself,"[45] [46][47][48] important other(s),[49][50][51] or special pet(s).[52][53][54] Direct your mind to focus on memories of experiencing the feeling of *acceptance* by doing an inner memory search through self-suggestion.[55] Experiencing or understanding the feelings is the most important aspect of this practice.

You may choose to say to yourself, "Let the... 'my' unconscious mind remember a time in the near or distant past when I felt a feeling of *acceptance.* Dwell upon that memory until that feeling of *acceptance* is bridged from the past sense of time to the 'my' immediate present awareness and feel the (immediately pleasurable) positive feeling of *acceptance.* Feel it 'from a little bit to a whole lot.'" This would be the *healing feeling.*

Practice saying to yourself, "I am determined to develop an *attitude*[56] of *healthy* self-*acceptance* to *accomplish* a more fulfilling life."[57] Many individuals remember a loving grandmother, others a neighbor, and others only a pet. The positive memory is a tool to re-experience the positive feeling, which begins or enhances one's foundation of confidence and happiness.[58]

Initially it is best to keep the exercise simple and basic. If you are blocking a memory of *acceptance* (often due to conflict or past trauma),[59] focus on a childhood pet such as a puppy and ask if the feeling of *acceptance* is then felt which is positive, "a little bit to a whole lot," 50+ percent of the time.

Later additions can be recollections of being *appreciated*; memories of *accomplishments, amusements,* and *awakening* to new ideas[60] [61] or experiences; and moments of *awe* of the *awesomeness* of nature and life.[62] Also after you have begun to master this learning, you will creatively add positive emotions of your own.

In the beginning, you may not feel some of the listed healing feelings. Nevertheless, continue with the others, and these particular feelings will eventually occur for all feelings are biological and variably felt consciously or unconsciously. Each emotion is variable in positive or negative intensity and frequency.[63] An ego building technique is a mental tool that can be used to further develop your own positive emotional or cognitive self-system as well as a therapeutic tool[64] with willing patients, family, or co-workers. Self-esteem is built more on positive feelings than positive concepts, but both are needed.[65]

Emotions are more powerful than cognition and come first in evolutionary development.[66] Cognition is like the rider of a horse (of emotions and behaviors) who trains, guides, waters, and feeds it, eventually for the rider's needs. Horses do best with positive domination when the rider loves the horse and the horse the rider.[67] [68] You want to train your emotions to love you and you to love your positive emotions. Then later, "without doubt" when you apply positive feelings to negative ones, they will soften and be less intense and (more) short lived. This will be realized only if you practice a training technique like this one. These techniques are mental tools to be used internally. The more tools a carpenter has, the more he can do.[69] Anthropologists calculate that man began to use external tools over two million years ago.[70] Nevertheless, the use of an external tool requires an internal mechanism to use it.[71] [72]

## SHIP

The second example is as follows:

The *core* of the ABCs is the healing concept of the *safe healing inner place* (SHIP). This concept comes under the healing letter "S" for *security*,[73] [74] *sacred*,[75] [76] *safety*, etc.

This feeling can best be felt at the center of the breath by noticing and mentally dwelling on a pause in the breath (breath pause) after breathing out and just before breathing in. This is when the autonomic nervous system is more in the parasympathetic than sympathetic "fight-flight" physiological state. This is when the natural sense of relaxation and peace is spontaneously and pleasantly felt.[77] [78] [79] Cat lovers go into synchrony with their cat into their own parasympathetic relaxation and peace when their cat is purring in its parasympathetic state of its relaxation and peace. The cat's feelings of rest and peace is infectious to cat lovers everywhere due to the bridge of feeling, in which an immediate positive pleasurable feeling is experienced by those in rapport with their pet cats.[80] [81] [82]

This *breath pause* is also called the expiratory pause. It is sometimes associated with feelings of tenderness and gentleness. Tenderness is often seen in the loving looking of mothers gently nursing their babies. Their breathing is generally slow and with momentary expiratory pauses. Onlookers will, often in sympathetic identification, say, "How precious!" as they too feel the tender elation, especially previously nursing mothers. It is now known that the brain hormone involved in this enhanced positive emotion is oxytocin. It is one of the several pleasure neurotransmitters.[83] The identification by the identifier is now known to be due to "mirror neurons" in the brain of the observer, and it is "as if the observer is doing the nursing herself."[84]

If this *rest and peace* is not immediately felt, try the following well-known technique: Take ten (10) relaxed breaths and focus on the breath pause to develop a pleasurable feeling in your *safe healing inner place* from a little bit to a whole lot. All that is needed is "a little bit," for repeated practice reinforces the feeling and in time develops new or strengthens existing connections (synapses) along positive pathways (dendrites) in the mood centers of your brain. This may take three (3) to six (6) months for the new nerve protoplasm (membranes, neurotransmitters, and receptors) to grow or be modified to create new positive connections (synapses).[85] Thus, new positive habits develop of feeling, most of the time, a sense of wholesomeness or well-being.[86]

Next, after focusing on and feeling the *breath pause* at the *center of breath* or any personal practice that works, begin the rest of the ABC techniques and feel each *healing feeling* at the center of the *safe healing inner place* "from a little bit to a whole lot" as best you can during each practice. Learn to let it happen, don't make it happen. Imagine it, visualize it happening, and after a little time, it will come to you automatically.[87 88 89 90 91]

# B

"B" is the next *healing letter*, and for the initial selected *healing word* is *belonging*. The *healing concept* is *belonging* to myself and/or important others or special pet(s).[92] Do an *inner memory search* and identify a memory(ies) of an experience of a feeling of *belonging*. Let yourself feel this feeling from "a little bit to a whole lot." After feeling this healing feeling, go to the next healing feeling.

Examples are as follows:

"I will every day remember times when I felt I *belonged* (to someone or group of friends or family)."[93][94][95]

"I shall dwell on the times I have felt *blessed*[96] by a *beautiful* uplifting moment observing the *beauty* of nature."[97][98]

"I remember by searching inward a feeling of being *beloved* (by someone or a special pet)."

"I will begin to remember and count my *beautiful beloved blessings.*"

# C

"C" is the *healing letter* for the *healing word* of *caring*. The *healing concept* is to "care for myself or significant others."[99][100] Do an *inner memory search* and remember being cared for or caring for someone or some pet.

Dwell on the memory until the feeling is automatically bridged from the past and felt in the present. Feel it "from a little bit to a whole lot," then go to the next *healing feeling*.

Examples are as follows:

"I remember the feeling of being *cared* for by (name the one(s) in your family)."

"I remember *caring* and being *cared* for by (name the friend[s])."

"I am beginning to learn to *care* for myself, important others, and acquaintances in a positive healthy way more each day."

"I am reminding myself that balanced *caring* for others is also *caring* for myself."

"I am becoming *contented*[101][102] when I experience a *caring compassion*[103][104][105][106] for myself and others."[107]

"I am developing a *cherishing*,[108] *caressing*,[109] comprehensive, contented, compassionate consciousness.*"

"I am *choosing* to develop an attitude of *compassionate curiosity*[110][111][112] about myself, others, and all that is positive that I know."

# D

"D" is for *deserving*, the next *healing word*. "I am a *deserving* person. I *deserve* to get better or [weller]" would be the *healing concept*.[113] Again dwell on an *inner memory search* and recollect a memory or memories relevant to this *healing concept* and do a *bridge of feelings* to the present to enjoy this HF before going to the next HF.

You can stop and start, as you need to; and if you have limited time, do only a few. You may skip one that is too difficult at the present and save for a later day. Also, you may do any one over and over. You may change the *healing word* (HW) and thus the *healing feeling* to one more specific to building your ego strengths[114] and/or the *healing concept* so long as it is universally *positive*.

The use of the abbreviations will now be used only when needed. Examples are as follows:

"I *deserve* to exist because a greater something [Mysterium Tremendum] *desired*[115] to create me."

"I *deserve* to be happier in life."[116][117][118]

"I remember earning and *deserving* (name the experience here)."

"I am worthy of *desiring* and *deserving* a better life."

"I *deserve* and *desire* to be a better person."[119][120]

"I *desire* a *dedicated*,[121][122] *devoted*,[123][124] *divine*[125][126][127] *direction* to a *heavenly healing*."

# E

"E" is for *enjoyment*,[128][129][130] *enhancing enjoyment, enjoying every day, experiencing enthusiasm*,[131][132] *enhancing energy, enthusiastic energy, energetic enthusiasm*, etc.

Examples are the following:

"I am beginning to find more *enjoyment* in my life and remember moments when I experienced enjoyment."

"I will let myself cherish this feeling of *happy elation* over and over until it is with me most of the time."

"I want to awaken with this feeling *enjoyable energy* every day."

"I shall *enhance*[133] and 'lift up' my life and others every moment I become aware and *deserve* to feel *enjoyment* in the presence of my *safe healing inner place*."

"I am determined to develop positive *enduring*[134][135] *endearing*[136] self-esteem."

"I am growing an attitude to *expect* and anticipate getting more *enjoyment* out of life every day."

# F

"F" is for *forgiveness*.[137][138]

"I will begin to feel *forgiving feelings*."

"I will initially remember only positive memories when I feel the feeling of *forgiveness*."

"At a later time but not now, I will use the *enhanced* feeling of *forgiveness* to heal the injuries that have created grudges that have eaten away at me."

"I will dwell on the positive forgiving experiences, either me forgiving another or another forgiving me, until I am strong enough to work on the unforgiving memories."

Forgiveness is the most treasured and the most treacherous of all spiritual sentiments.

Begin to develop a *forgiving faith*[139][140] and a *faithful forgiving*. No one can escape the felt vengeance when done wrong. Everyone has a laundry list of personal injuries from slights to catastrophes. All can eat away at one's soul and create an ongoing miserable hell on earth. They can be like parasites that suck the positive life out of one's existence.[141]

*"Forgiveness does not change the past,*
*but it does enlarge the future."*
*(Paul Boese, 1923-1976)*

Months from now, you may choose to deliberately collect memories of minor vengeance.

Then, bring them one at a time slowly over time to your SHIP after you have felt more than twice as much forgiveness before bringing the negative grudge to be desensitized and blended with all the *positive* HF you can feel. You will be surprised with a HF of *relief.*

To clarify the above, start with remembering minor memories of vengeance and make a tolerable list that does not stir up too much negativity. Then, when you have enough emotional ego strength, deliberately collect a list of your memories and feelings of forgiveness. Then, practice them one by one in your *safe healing inner place* (SHIP). You must have two or more positive feelings to begin to subdue each negative one. I encourage several. When you feel you are ready, bring only one minor selected memory of a desire to retaliate and feel the selected minor negative and greater positive feelings together at or near the same time. This will dilute and blend the feeling of revenge with forgiving feelings and gradually relegate that particular negative feeling to just a memory with maybe minor sadness. This process with variations can be used sequentially with your list of grudges until you feel relieved of these hurts most of the time.

I mention sadness, for there will be a grief response as you give up and overcome each negative attachment. It is a process. You cannot *forgive* and *forget* for your unconscious will not let you. You must *remember* and *forgive.* Grief is our most painful *normal feeling,* and it lasts longer than childbirth for a mother.

For example, "I shall do an inner memory search to find as many experiences of the relief (immediate positive experience) of *forgiving* someone who injured me or being *forgiven* by another that I have offended."

Forgiveness does not mean that misbehavior, criminal or evil behavior, should be condoned or go without punishment. Nor does it mean that after someone is forgiven, one should permit anyone to repeatedly re-injure you or others.[142]

Other positive *feelings* may be *feeling faith;*[143] *feeling faithful; feeling fascination*[144] [145] with oneself, others, and all that is positive; and *feeling* more *free* inside.[146]

17

# G

"G" is for *goodness*[147] and for the *getting* and *giving* of *goodness* to oneself and/or one another;[148] the *getting* and *giving* of *gratitude*,[149] [150] *gracious goodness*; or remembering the feeling of *gratitude*,[151] *gratitude* for the *greatness* of the *gift* of *life*, the *goodness* of *gratitude*, *gratitude* for the feeling of *goodness*, of *gracefulness*, the *guidance* of *grace*.[152] [153]

Recollect and repeat the forgoing healing words and healing concepts during this ego building exercise to internalize the healing feelings over time.

The following are examples:

"I will remember precious memories of when I was *good* to someone and when someone was *good* to me and feel this feeling every day until I feel it most of the time."

"I remember when I first felt *grace* and in remembering I feel it all over, again."

"I am going to remember and feel *gracefulness* every day."

"I will nourish my feeling of *gratitude* and thankfulness every moment I become aware of the *gift* of *graciousness*."

# H

"H" is for *hope*,[154] [155] *healing hope, hopeful healing*,[156] *heavenly healing happiness, healing humility*,[157] [158] *healing humor*,[159] [160] [161] *healing heart, happiness.* [162] [163] [164] [165]

Focus your attention on as many experiences of *hope* as you can, and the list will grow with practice. Let your heart feel this healing feeling, which becomes a seed that grows in the *healing heart*[166] of your *soul* and flowers perennially. Many have happy memories of a pet dog when returning home from school or work. Most of the time, there is a near unconditional joyful happy acceptance by the dog when its master is expected. This experience infectiously resonates joy and happiness in most dog lovers.

*"The more I get to know about*
*people the more I like my dog."*
*(Mark Twain, 1835-1910)*

Below are examples:

"I will let my mind concentrate on memories of feeling *hope* and *happiness* and feel them over and over until I feel them all the time almost."

"Let me reminisce on the *healing feeling* which I would feel when getting over an illness, *healing hope, hopeful healing,* or a hurt *healing heart* and how *good* it felt. I want to nurture these HF until they are with me when I need them."

Other positive feelings may be *healing humor, humane healing,* and *healing holy hope.*[167]

# I

"I" is for *intelligence,*[168] [169] [170] *inner intelligence, increasing inner intelligence, intuition,*[171] *intuitive intelligence, intelligent intuition, increasing intelligent intuition,*[172] *increasing inner importance, increasing inner important intelligent intuitive ideas of identity,*[173] [174] *intensely increasing inner intelligence,* etc.[175]

All intelligence come through the inner mechanisms of our central nervous system, but it needs stimulation from the outside, through our senses, and from the inside, by intuition, inner creative imagination,[176] curiosity, rational thought, and fantasy.[177] [178] [179] [180] Become aware of your inner intelligent creative problem-solving abilities, and let them develop in your conscious consciousness and your conscious unconsciousness. One of the recent theories of at least one function of dreams during sleep is that our unconscious mind is mulling over problems of the day and lifelong problems to solve them during the next day.[181] [182]

Examples are below:

"My inner intelligence is increasing each time I remember forgotten positive memories."

"Each time I learn a new way of feeling a healing feeling is an increase in my inner intelligence."

"I am increasing my self-importance by giving myself positive feelings that I deserve."

"Positive feelings and ideas seem to come from nowhere as my positive intuition grows."

# J

"J" is for *journey…journey of joy,*[183] [184] [185] *joyfulness…*

"My *life* is becoming more, and more a *joyful journey* as I feel more, and more often the healing feelings."

"It is *just* that I feel *joy* and *happiness*."

All animals appear happy unless pursued by a predator, fighting for a mate, physically sick, hungry, or thirsty. We are made to be *joyful.* For a fact, we have internal natural morphine-like hormones that give us our joyful well-being. They are known as endorphins, and it is nature's way, perhaps God's way, of giving us *joyfulness.* It is a fact that those who are more *joyful* have healthier immune systems.[186]

Examples are below mentioned:

"I am suggesting to myself to remember *joyful* memories several times every day."

"I am beginning to deliberately remember *joyful* memories and feelings when I am disappointed, hurt, or saddened."

"No matter what has happened in the past or what will happen in the future, I will remind myself to remember the positive memories as often as needed to preserve a *joyful happy* outlook in my life."[187] [188]

"I am learning more with each step on my *journey* to a *joyful* life the importance of *practicing* the *positive healing feelings.*"[189]

# K

"K" is for *kindness,*[190] [191] [192] *knowledge of kindness, knowing the inner kingdom of kindness,* etc.

Make your inner life a *kingdom* of *kindness.* Kindness is non-possessive where *love* can be. *Kindness* is often shown to strangers and *love* to important others. *Kindness* does not deplete the giver where *love* can. *Kindness* is more akin to agape love. Begin to be *kind* to yourself, and it will be easy to be *kind* to all life. *Kindness* creates a *joy* all its own. Begin to practice an attitude and feeling of *loving kindness*[193] toward yourself and others as if all are eternal souls in and a part of the (*Mystery That Is* and the *All That Is*), and *loving kindness* in a short time will come to stay.

Examples are the following:

"Let my unconscious bring to awareness recollections of *kindness* toward myself and when I was kind to someone and feel how it felt."

"I am *increasingly enjoying* my memories of *kindness*. It is like counting my *blessings*."

## L

"L" is for *love*,[194] [195] [196] a *loving looking* at myself, *learning* a *lasting loyal*[197] [198] *compassionate*[199] [200] *loving*[201] toward myself and others, an *agape*[202] [203] *love*[204] [205] to share with myself and others in people-ship (fellowship and sister-ship),[206] *longing* to *live life lovingly*, *learning* to *love lastingly*, *longing* for *lasting love*, *learning lasting lessons* of *love*, etc.

*Love* is a highly charged word with variable meanings. It needs adjectives to qualify the expression and impression. Nevertheless, we *long*[207] for its feeling if we have had a lot or not enough. One is fortunate if one has had enough non-possessive *love* to be able to *love* others non-possessively. This type of *love* enriches and blends with all the positive healing feelings and strengthens and solidifies one's *core safe healing inner place*. When your "cup runneth over" with *loving kindness* like the purr of a cat, it stimulates synchrony, resonance, and its growth in others.

Examples are as follows:

"I will *learn* to look at myself in a more *loving* way."

"Every day when I look in the mirror, I shall begin to look at myself with a *loving looking*."

"I remember how mothers have a mutual *loving looking* with their baby[208] and feel that feeling with myself."

"I remind myself to look at my loved ones with a *loving looking*."

"I shall *learn* to have a *kind loving looking* at myself."

"I am *learning* to develop a non-possessive *love* toward myself and others."

"I will begin to nurture an agape *love* to share with myself and others in people-ship, fellowship and sister-ship."

"I am deciding to practice and fill my inner cup with a *loving kindness* until it spills over."

# M

"M" is for *motivation*,[209] *mastery*,[210] *motivation of a mission*[211] *to master* oneself *more, more motivation* to *master* and feel my *healing feelings*.

The *miracle* of my *mirroring mind*[212][213][214] is to *master* my *motivation* of positive *emotions, marveling* the *Mystery of Life—motivation* to *move* to a *more meaningful mission* in life.

"I will remember times when I felt *motivated* to accomplish a project or task and succeeded. I will feel that *motivation* to continue to *master* the ABCs."

"With each healing practice of the *healing feelings*, I come closer to *mastering* the ABCs and strengthening my *safe healing inner place*."

"It is my *mission* to feel the sum of the healing feelings most of the time and when not doing so to focus my awareness on the SHIP and begin to load each *healing feeling* on board one at a time until my positive attitude and emotional state are more than 51 percent stronger than my negative ones."

"Each day as I practice feeling the *healing feelings*, I become *more motivated* to feel them more."

"*Minding* the *mystery* of *awakening* to the *awareness* that I can *master* the ABCs in time."

"*Appreciating* the *awesomeness* of the *Mystery of Life* gives me the *motivation* to *move* on to a better *more* positive life."[215]

# N

"N" is about nurturing inner healing. For *noticing* positive *normal* feelings and *new notions*[216][217] *of self-nurture.*[218]

"I am *noticing* more and more each day *normal* positive healing feelings and learning *new notions* how to grow my inner self in my *safe healing inner places* and become a more *happy* and *peaceful* person."

"I am *noticing new* ways to think and positively feel more forgotten healing feeling as I concentrate on my inner memory searches."

"I am learning to *nurture new normal* positive healing feelings and ignore unnecessary negative ones."

## O

"O" is for *openness,*[219][220] *open origination,*[221] *openness to opportunities, openness to original opportunities,*[222] etc.

"I am *open* to *opportunities* to *originate oneness* with all of my positive emotions every time I have an *opportunity* to *notice* them."

*Openness* to the positive does not eliminate the negative but is an *opportunity* to *master* your negative emotions and use them in their rational time and place. *Openness* is *originating new* ways to experience positive healing feelings and an *opportunity* to subdue irrational negative feelings. After several months, your ABCs will have been internalized as a permanent memory system, just as permanent as your memory of the alphabet.[223] You can then *carefully* recall an initial list of a few of, at first, minor damaging negative feeling you have experienced and then introduce each with two or preferably more *healing feelings* in your *safe feeling inner place*. This will begin to compete with and inhibit the negative feelings with the positive emotions by bringing one of the unruly negative feelings one by one into the *safe healing inner place* to be diluted by desensitization and then reined under your rational control.

Say to yourself or something positive in your own way similar to the following self-suggestions:

"I will learn to become *more open* to *originating* new solutions to create a *wholesome oneness*[224] in myself to lead a more *contented meaningful* life."[225][226][227]

"I will be *more open* to the positive in others and be more positive emotionally toward them."

Both negative and positive feelings are biological given and have their purpose in our self and species preservation.[228] If an infant were not greedy, the infant would not survive, and in this aspect greed is positive. Excessive greed, as an adult, is socially negative and has consequences. Envy is a later greed for other's possessions and motivates initially growth for acquisitions and later may be sublimated by admiration to a "lust for knowledge," job or professional achievement, and music or artistic career. Everyone knows the consequences of excessive greed in our families, communities, and society. Fear and anger have their place as well.

Negative emotions tend to be specific and narrow one's awareness toward a specific object. The nervous system becomes aroused in the flight-fight mode, and the sympathetic system is excited by adrenalin. The central nervous system is also excited by an increase in glutamate, an excitatory neuropeptide. Fear, envy, jealousy, anger, and other negative emotions narrow our attention in the direction of relevant specific targets. The so-called negative emotions have both negative and positive aspects, and it requires mature insight, as well as judiciousness to discern the difference and proper use of each for your own self-preservation and for your family and society.

Positive emotions are less specific and tend to blend together as you will progressively experience them. Feelings of *caring, forgiveness, gratitude, kindness, peace,* and other positive feelings blend as you begin to have a generalized *well-being* and *loving kindness* of *happiness.* Yet if you are not *careful* of protecting your boundaries, there are emotionally undeveloped individuals and organizations that will invade and destroy or take away your emotional or physical wealth. Thus, positive emotions can also be misused negatively. On the positive side, one of the significant benefits of *enhanced happiness* is that it *opens up* and *broadens* your mind to more *choices* and *opportunities* in decision-making. Instead of one specific *choice* when in a negative protective state, you will soon see, due to *broadening* and *opening* your awareness, several more *choices* or *opportunities* will be available to you in your life.

## P

"P" is for *peacefulness, purposely pursuing the presence of peace, purposefully pursuing peaceful places, precious peace, peaceful preciousness, peaceful purpose, purpose of peace, practice of peace,* etc.

"I am *pursuing* the *presence* of *peace* by remembering one by one my *precious* memories of the experiences of *peace*."

"I am *pursuing* an inner *place* of *peace* on *purpose* in my *safe healing inner place*."

"I will find time for *peace time* every day in my SHIP."

"I shall become in time a *peacemaker* and a *peacemaster* for myself and others."

"I am learning to be *at peace* with myself, with others, and the world which I cannot change."

"I shall with *purposeful practice* find *the peace* in my *purposeful life* in my *heart* in my *serene safe healing inner precious peaceful presence.*"[229][230][231][232]

## Q

"Q" is for a *quest*[233][234] for inner *quietness, quietude,*[235][236][237][238] *quest* for a life of *quality*, a vision *quest* to develop an inner *precious quiet peace* and *happiness*.

"The more I feel the inner *quietness*, the more I *journey* on my *quest* for *perfect* inner *peace*."

"My *quietude* is my *quiet quest* to *overcome* my limiting negative emotions and cognitions."[239]

"*Quiet* words and thoughts to myself and others turn away the negative in my life more often to enhance the *quality* of my *life*."[240][241]

## R

"R" is for *rejoicing,*[242][243][244] *recollections of rejoicing, remembering to relax and rest,*[245] *remembering recreations, remembering recollections of rest and recuperation, remembering of rejoicing, rejoicing joyfulness, recollecting* memories of *recreational rejuvenation*, etc.

"*Rest* is necessary to *restore* my energy to do my healing work, to *repair* the wear and tear of my life's work."

"It is easy to *remember* times of *rejoicing* and *recreation*."

"I *recreate rejuvenation* by *remembering* early experience of *recreation*."

To *re-experience restfulness and relaxation* of your muscles, try doing the commonly known exercises of successive *relaxing* of each part of your body starting with your toes and working your way to your head and face. This is a commonly known exercise practice, the Jacobson's progressive relaxation technique.[246][247][248][249][250]

# S

"S" is for *safe healing inner place* (SHIP)[251] to *feel* all the *healing feelings* at the center of your breath. Initially this may be experienced one at a time as you go through the ABCs, which is recommended. Months later, you will experience a blending of many, if not all, positive feelings you have been practicing by just focusing your attention on your *center of your breath* and thinking or saying to yourself, "Feel my *safe healing inner place*" or "SHIP." You may choose to use visual imagery and visualize a large sailing ship and imagine loading each healing feelings on board one at a time.

SHIP can also represent a *secure helping intelligent presence*,[252] *sacred heavenly intuitive peace*, *sacred healing inner presence*,[253][254][255] or any positive variation.

The purpose of developing the SHIP is to link (gather together) all the positive feelings you have been experiencing. In doing so, you eventually can almost immediately feel a blended swelling *enjoyable euphoria* at any time without anyone knowing. If you choose to share how you do this, be selective and judicious for there will be a few who are ignorant who may use your personal knowledge to attack you.

Another purpose is to use the SHIP or selected HFs to desensitize and heal old negative memories and feelings. When you have enough *mastery* of the ABCs, I recommend that you make a list of your negative experiences and prioritize them.

Initially in a secure private environment, go through the ABCs one at a time in your SHIP. Then carefully recall one of the lesser painful experiences while maintaining the positive feelings in the SHIP. When the negative feelings diminish a "little bit," stop and repeat this technique with intervals of more than one–two hours apart. This process will in time desensitize the particular negative feeling to a minimum or manageable level of intensity.[256][257][258][259]

Later, when you have *mastered* the visualization of your image of a ship or your image of choice and immediately feel the blended feelings and *enjoyable euphoria* in your consciousness of the presence of your SHIP, you are then, when you are ready, encouraged to use this mental tool to withstand most of the stressors and crises in your life. For example, you may get into an insignificant quarrel with your significant other and get an angry feeling. This type of anger is often nonproductive. You can choose to rapidly diminish this negative emotion in this situation by diverting and directing your focused attention to the image of the ship or your image of choice as your symbol to bring your SHIP from your unconscious consciousness to your conscious consciousness. Then you can begin to feel one or many blended positive feelings, which are your ABCs. Of course as discussed before, there are positive uses of anger when it is necessary to protect yourself or loved one(s).

# T

"T" is for *thankfulness*,[260][261][262] *tender tactfully*[263][264] *truthfulness*,[265] *trusting*[266] *thankfulness, tender tactful thoughtfulness*,[267][268] *thoughtful thankfulness, therapeutic thankfulness, tenderly timely tactfully trusting truthfulness*, etc.

"I am *thankful* for the positive feeling I can feel at will by concentrating on a positive memory."

"I am becoming more *tenderly therapeutically timely truthful* toward myself."

"I am learning to be more *tactfully thoughtfully truthful* with relevant others."

# U

"U" is for *understanding*,[269] *understanding a united understanding, understanding unity, useful understanding.*[270]

"I am beginning to *understand* how the ABCs all fit together."

"I am learning to *understand* more about *understanding* the *unification* of the *healing feelings* of the ABCs."

"I am *uniting* the *useful* positive *healing feelings* in my *safe healing inner place* one by one, day by day."

"I am *understanding* my *inner intelligence* more every day."[271]

# V

"V" is for *vision*,[272] *visualization* of the *victory of mastering* the ABCs.

"As I begin to *master* the *healing feelings*, I am beginning to feel the beginning of a feeling of *victory.*"

"I am becoming more in emotional control of myself as I see my *vision* of learning to be *happy* most of the time."

Select a symbol to *visualize* as a beacon of *victory*, such as a warm safe candlelight, star in the night, or a selected safe outer place.[273][274]

# W

"W" is for *wellness, wanting wellness, wishing well-being, willingness* to *work* to get *weller*,[275] *wanting wisdom, working* with *wisdom*[276] to become *wholesome.*[277]

"I *want* to be *weller* and *wholesome* every *opportunity* when I remind myself."

"I am *willing* to *work* on myself more *wisely* with the *new notions* I have with my *increasing inner intelligence*, to become more *worthy* and *wise.*"

"I am *working* on *increasing* my *enjoyable euphoria* in my *well-being.*"

# X

"X" is for an *extraordinary intelligent presence* to unconsciously guide and give you the consciousness of the *healing feelings.*

You may choose to call this God, *divine presence, higher power, the unconscious mind, inner nature,* or what you wish. Nevertheless, there is an "X" factor, an *Awesome Mystery, a "Mysterium Tremendum et Fascinains" Rudolph Otto (1869-1937)* that accounts for the healing process. Though *It* is *ever present* when *Its* presence is felt, there is ever a much more powerful healing.

"I *wish* to become more *aware* of this *force* and learn to be partners with *It* as I become *weller* and *weller.*"

"I am *willing* to *work* with my *unconscious mind* to autosuggest the *healing feelings* I *want.*"

"I, in the *presence* of *God,* will ask *him* to help me feel the *healing feelings* to *heal* my *soul.*"[278][279]

# Y

"Y" is for *yearning* to get *weller, yearning*[280][281] to become *joyful* most of the time, a *yes attitude.*

"I am learning a *yes attitude*[282] that I can *master* the *healing feelings* and *enhance* my life and those around me."

"I *yearn* for the *victory* of *mastering* the ABCs of *healing feelings* in my life and for the rest of my life.

# Z

"Z" is for *zeal, zeal* with the urgent effort to get *weller, zest* with fiery *determination* to *master* the positive feelings of the ABCs.[283][284]

"I am *dedicated* to *mastering* with *zest* the harnessing of my mind by *working wisely* and with a *united understanding* of the ABCs."[285][286][287]

"I am *determined* with urgent *zeal* to *overcome* any obstacle in the way of my *vision* of *victory* over my limiting negative feelings and thoughts."

After each practice of the healing feelings, repeat the following promises.

# THE SEVEN HEALING PROMISES TO GET WELLER

**W**hy the promises? Many do not do what is best for themselves until they make commitments to do so.

1. I promise myself and my loved ones to begin to get "weller and weller."
   (To get as well as I can, soon as I can.)
2. I promise to begin to be tenderly and tactfully truthful to myself and others that I trust, only at the right time, at the right place, and the right amount (not too little or too much). Too much too soon may be overwhelming and psychologically un-digestible.
3. I promise to be truthful only in a healing way to myself and to others that I trust at the right time and place and right amount when ready to receive. Sometimes,

> *"The truth told with ill intent beats*
> *all the lies you can invent"*
> *(William Blake, 1757-1827)*

4. I promise to begin to cause no harm to myself or others, inside myself or outside myself, at any time or any place, for any reason, except to protect my loved ones and myself.
5. I promise to begin to be happy most of the time; to get happy as soon as possible when I am unhappy, not at the expense of others; and to help others learn to be happy, if I can and they are ready to learn.

6. I promise to feel the *healing feelings* over and over until they are automatically being felt most of the time and to feel them as quick as I can, except when I must protect my loved ones and/or myself.

7. I promise to begin to keep my promises and to practice the ABCs of *healing feelings* with the *determination* of *zest* and *zeal.*

Signature_____    Date ___/___/_____

(Your signature is an honest commitment to all of yourself, conscious and unconscious, implicit and explicit to improve your life to the best of your ability.)[288 289 290 291 292]

Ronald L. Kelley, MD, DLFAPA (*Distinguished Life Fellow American Psychiatric Association*)

It is recommended that you practice Version I. A. one to two months before practicing Version I. B. or Version I. C. Later when practicing Version I. B. or I. C., you may need to return to Version I. A. when you have sufficient time or need.

The ABCs of Healing Feelings; The Alphabet of Healing Feelings, aka;
The ABCs/Alphabet of Happiness/Happy/Healthy Feelings,
The ABCs/Alphabet of Wellbeing/Wellness/Wellerness/
Wholesomeness/Wholesome Feelings,
The ABCs/Alphabet of Self Esteem/Serenity/Peacefulness/
Positivity/Optimism/Contentment/Compassion,
Ronald L. Kelley, M.D., Distinguished Life Fellow
American Psychiatric Association
Copyright 2014

# ABCS OF HEALING FEELING, VERSION I. B.

After you begin to thoroughly understand Version I. A., this section is a simplified version that can be practiced in less time. Also you are encouraged to begin to list as many different memories of each *positive feeling memory* as you can. You will find that more and more are remembered as you go along over time. As you accumulate more memories, you will find that the strength of the positive feelings will grow and last longer. It will change your brain for the rest of your life for the better.

"A" is for acceptance, an *acceptance* of one's self and one another. Let the unconscious remember a time in the past when a part of the unconscious felt a feeling of *acceptance*. Bridge that feeling from the past to the present consciousness, and feel an immediate pleasurable experience of *acceptance*.

1. _____. 2. _____. 3. _____. Etc.

"B" is for *belonging*, a feeling of *belonging* to one's self and one another inside. Let the unconscious remember from a past conscious experience the positive feeling of *belonging*. Bring this feeling emotion of *belonging* into the present awareness, and immediately feel it, even if it is a small amount or a large amount.

1. _____. 2. _____. 3. _____. Etc.

"C" is for *caring*, a *caring* for one's self and others. Remember a feeling of *caring* in the past. When the memory is recalled, bring the *caring*, healing feeling to the present mind and enjoy it.

    1. _____. 2. _____. 3. _____. Etc.

"D" is for *deserving—deserving* to get well. Let a *deserving* feeling come from a past memory. Transfer the feeling of *deserving* into the present and give it to yourself.

    1. _____. 2. _____. 3. _____. Etc.

"E" is for *energy*, a healing *energy* to get well. Remember a time when you had an abundance of *energy*. Bring this *energetic* feeling to the present awareness and channel it for you to get well.

    1. _____. 2. _____. 3. _____. Etc.

"F" is for *faith*, a healing *faith* to get well. Again recall a feeling of *faith*. Bring it to your present experience.

    1. _____. 2. _____. 3. _____. Etc.

"G" is for *goodness*, a *giving* of *goodness* to one's self and one another. Remember the pleasure of *getting* and *giving goodness* sometime in the past and give it to the present conscious state.

    1. _____. 2. _____. 3. _____. Etc.

"H" is for *hope*, a helpful, healing *hope* to get well. Remember a time of *hopefulness*. Bring the feeling of *hopefulness* to the present to help with the healing inside.

    1. _____. 2. _____. 3. _____. Etc.

"I" is for *intelligence*, an increasing inner *intelligence* to get well. Recall how the inner consciousness has felt with the growing feeling of *intelligence*. Bring that feeling to the present, to know how to get well more quickly.

    1. _____. 2. _____. 3. _____. Etc.

"J" is for *journey*, a healing *journey* to get well. Remember taking a *journey* somewhere that was satisfying and fulfilling. Bring that sense of a healing, satisfying *journey* to mind, and see the beginning to get well.

1. _____. 2. _____. 3. _____. Etc.

"K" is for *kindness*, a healing *kindness* toward one's self and others. Let the mind remember a past feeling of *kindness*. Bring it to the present awareness.

1. _____. 2. _____. 3. _____. Etc.

"L" is for *longing*, a growing *longing* to get well. Remember any memory of a *longing* feeling. Bring that longing feeling into the here and now.

1. _____. 2. _____. 3. _____. Etc.

"M" is for *mission*, a healing *mission* to get well. Remember any purposeful *mission*, and bring that sense of *mission* in the here and now.

1. _____. 2. _____. 3. _____. Etc.

"N" is for *normalcy*, a healing, natural *normal* experience. Remember a time when you felt a *normal*, new experience, and bring that experienced feeling into the new awareness and let all feel it.

1. _____. 2. _____. 3. _____. Etc.

"O" is for *openness*, an *openness* to getting well. Let yourself remember an *open* feeling where you learned something new and exciting. Then feel it in the present.

1. _____. 2. _____. 3. _____. Etc.

"P" is for *peacefulness*, a healing, precious inner *peacefulness* while getting well. Let a *peace* from the past be remembered and brought into the consciousness of the present.

1. _____. 2. _____. 3. _____. Etc.

"Q" is for *quietness,* an inner healing *quietness.* Find a memory of a *quiet* spot and feeling.

  1. _____. 2. _____. 3. _____. Etc.

"R" is for *recovery,* a sense of healing *recovery* as you get well. Recall a time you *recovered* from an illness, and bring that feeling of *recovery* to the present consciousness.

  1. _____. 2. _____. 3. _____. Etc.

"S" is for SHIP, the building of a *safe,* healing inner place. Remember or create an inner feeling of *safety, security,* and *strength,* and feel these feelings now. Begin to put all of the healing feelings in the *safe,* healing inner place. Now feel the *safe,* healing inner place. The mission of the SHIP is *sincere, seeking,* and *searching* for all ways to get well.

  1. _____. 2. _____. 3. _____. Etc.

"T" is for *truth* and *trust,* a healing, *tender, truthful trust* toward one's self and one another as realistically understood. Remember a feeling of *truthfulness* and *truth.*

  1. _____. 2. _____. 3. _____. Etc.

"U" is for *understanding* and *unity,* a healing *understanding* of how to get well. Recall the times you have begun to *understand* something in your education or life experience, and bring that *understanding* feeling into the present. *Understanding* is *uniting.*

  1. _____. 2. _____. 3. _____. Etc.

"V" is for *visualization,* the *visualization* of beginning, becoming, and being well. Tell me when you see this picture. Good. It is also for a *vision* of *victory* over illness.

  1. _____. 2. _____. 3. _____. Etc.

"W" is for *worthiness*, a healing *worthiness* to get well. Tell me when you feel it. Good. Now feel the healing *wisdom* that makes the best decision to get well, as quick as possible with the least trouble and pain.

    1. _____. 2. _____. 3. _____. Etc.

"X" is for *extra*, an *extra* special, safe, healing inner place for all the healing feelings to grow.

    1. _____. 2. _____. 3. _____. Etc.

"Y" is for *yearning*, a *yearning* for all to stay in the safe, healing inner place at all times under all circumstances.

    1. _____. 2. _____. 3. _____. Etc.

"Z" is for *zeal*, the *zeal* of actualizing the awakening of the safe, healing inner place where the healing memories and feelings are found.

    1. _____. 2. _____. 3. _____. Etc.

# THE SEVEN HEALING PROMISES TO GET WELLER

1. I promise myself and my loved ones to begin to get "weller and weller."
   (To get as well as soon as I can.)
2. I promise to begin to be tenderly and tactfully truthful to myself and others that I trust, only at the right time, at the right place, and the right amount (not too little or too much). Too much too soon may be overwhelming and psychologically un-digestible.
3. I promise to be truthful only in a healing way to myself and to others that I trust at the right time and place and right amount when ready to receive.

> *"The truth told with ill intent*
> *beats all the lies you can invent"*
> *(William Blake, 1757-1827)*

4. I promise to begin to cause no harm to myself or others, inside myself or outside myself, at any time or any place, for any reason, except to protect my loved ones and myself.
5. I promise to begin to be happy most of the time; to get happy as soon as possible when I am unhappy, not at the expense of others; and to help others learn to be happy, if I can and they are ready to learn.
6. I promise to feel the *healing feelings* over and over until they are automatically being felt most of the time and to feel them as quick as I can, except when I must protect my loved ones and/ or myself.

7. I promise to begin to keep my promises and to practice the ABCs of *healing feelings* with the *determination* of *zest* and *zeal*.

Signature_____ Date ___/___/_____

(Your signature is an honest commitment to all of yourself, conscious and unconscious, implicit and explicit to improve your life to the best of your ability.)

The ABCs of Healing Feelings; The Alphabet of Healing Feelings, aka;

The ABCs/Alphabet of Happiness/Happy/Healthy Feelings,

The ABCs/Alphabet of Wellbeing/Wellness/Wellerness/ Wholesomeness/Wholesome Feelings,

The ABCs/Alphabet of Self Esteem/Serenity/Peacefulness/ Positivity/Optimism/Contentment/Compassion,

Ronald L. Kelley, M.D., Distinguished Life Fellow

American Psychiatric Association

Copyright 2014


The author gives you permission to copy for personal use pages 33 through 39 for the pursuit of your optimal wellbeing.

# ABCS OF HEALING
# FEELING VERSION I. C.

After the foregoing practices have been mastered enough and multiple positive associations have become networks of groups of associations in your brain, you can then simplify the practice of the ABCs of positive emotions (healing feelings).

When you stimulate one portion of this developing web of blending positive feelings, the entire web shakes with a feeling of happiness. This is truly a pursuit of happiness.

You may in your own way do the following by just going through the alphabet and say silently or out loud in private the healing words and begin to feel the blending happy feelings.

Always begin after you get in your SHIP. Gradually and eventually when you visualize a ship of your choice, you will immediately feel a *spontaneous happy immediate presence*. One very effective technique is to revive and feel one HF at the center of your breath pause consecutively from A to Z in 26 normal calm breaths in as little as three to five minutes.

*Feel one or two healing feelings of your choice and vary the healing feelings from time to time.*

"A"   *acceptance, awakened awareness of acceptance, awesome awareness of acceptance,* etc. (You may create your own variation with words beginning with the healing letter of "A.")

"B"   *belonging, beloved belonging, blessed belonging, belonging to a blessed being(s), being blessed with the breath of being,* etc. (Or create your own variation.)

40

"C"   *caring, compassion, compassionate caring, caressing caring, caring compassionate curiosity, compassionate consciousness, conscientious caring, charity,* etc.

"D"   *deserving, dwelling in deserving, deserving a divine direction, dedicated devotion (dedication* to become happier), *etc.*

"E"   *enjoyment, energy, endearment, exploring enjoyable esteem, exuberance, ecstasy, elation,* etc.

"F"   *forgiveness, faith, forgiving faith, faithful forgivingness, fascination with foreverness, finding forever in the fountain of forgiving faith and a faithful forgivingness,* etc.

"G"   *goodness, getting goodness, giving goodness, getting and giving goodness,* the *getting* and *giving of gratitude, gracious goodness; or remembering th*e feeling of *gratitude, gratitude* for the *greatness* of the gift of life, the *goodness* of *gratitude, gratitude* for the feeling of *goodness,* of *gracefulness,* the *guidance of grace.*

"H"   *hope, healing hopefulness, hopeful healing, healing humility, humaneness, humane healing, heavenly healing, honoring heavenly hope, healing happiness, healing humor,* etc.

"I"   *increasing inner intelligence, increasing inner identity, increasing inner inclusive identity, increasing inner intuitive ideas, increasing inner importance,* etc.

"J"   *journey of joy, journey of justice, joyful journey, jubilant journey, judicious joy,* etc.

"K"   *kindness, kingdom of kindness, knowledge of kindness, kindling the kingdom of kindness,* etc.

"L"   *loving looking, longing to love, lasting love, learning to love, loving light of love, longing loving light,* etc.

"M"   *more mastery, mission of mastery, more motivation, memories of mastery, mastering memories,* etc.

"N"   *needing normalness, noticing new normal needs, needing normal newness, new normal needs, normal new needs,* etc.

"O"   *openness, open to opportunities, open to optimistic opportunities, open to optimism, optimistic openness,* etc.

"P"   *peacefulness, pursuit of the presence of peace, pursuing peace, pursuing peaceful pleasure, pursuing peaceful purpose, pursuing positivity, persistent promotion of the presence of a precious positive peaceful pleasure, positive precious prayers, positive peaceful praise,* etc.

"Q"	*quietude, questing for quality, quality of quietness, quest for quiescence, quickening quiescence,* etc.

"R"	*resilience, reaching restfulness, relaxing recreation, recovery, renewal, rejuvenation, responsible reflection, respectfulness, respectful reflection, righteous reflection, resolution to reach resilience, relating righteously,* etc.

"S"	SHIP, *sailing* with a *safe healing inner place, seeking* and *searching* for all ways to get "weller," *strengthening serenity, seeking safe solutions, spontaneous smiling, serenity smiling, seeking security, seeking a spiritual holy illuminating presence,* SHIP *worthiness,* etc.

"T"	*tender truthfulness, truthful timeliness, truthful trustfulness, tenderly tactful truthfulness, therapeutic truthfulness, therapeutic trustworthiness, truthful thinking therapy, truthful tolerance, therapeutic theater of truthful thought,* etc.

"U"	*understanding, urgently understanding, unity, united understanding, united unconscious understanding, unchained united understanding, understanding unchained unity, unconstrained, utmost useful understanding,* etc.

"V"	*visualize victory, vison of vitality, validate vision of victory, vital vision of victory,* etc.

"W"	*worthiness* to get *well, willingness* to *work* to get *weller, worthy* of *wisdom, working* with *wisdom,* etc.

"X"	*x-tra focus* on the *un-x-plainable x-factor,* the *x-tra present, x-tra conscious, x-tra powerful, x-tra mystery* for *x-tra-ordinary x-tra x-tascy,* and *x-tra healing*

"Y"	*Yes! I have learned the ABCs by heart.*

"Z"	*zest, zeal, zeal* and *zest,* etc.

You will find that when you use this positive mental tool in the midst of adversity that you sail and captain the stormy seas of life with much greater success than before. Your mind will creatively open up more. You will broaden and build better relationships with yourself and others. You will be more open to more opportunities because of your improved perceptions in your positive problem-solving skills, and most importantly all your genuine happiness will begin to "run-neth over" for others to share.

After a few months, you can at any time experience one ABC feeling with each twenty-six consecutive breaths in less than four minutes without anyone knowing you are doing it. If you do this each waking morning, it will start your day with a resilient attitude, whether you will be in a safe harbor or stormy sea. You will *carpe diem*.

# THE SEVEN HEALING PROMISES TO GET WELLER

1.  I promise my loved ones and myself to begin to get "weller and weller."
    (To get as well as soon as I can.)
2.  I promise to begin to be tenderly and tactfully truthful to myself and others that I trust, only at the right time, at the right place, and the right amount (not too little or too much). Too much too soon may be overwhelming and psychologically un-digestible.
3.  I promise to be truthful only in a healing way to myself and to others that I trust at the right time and place and right amount when ready to receive.

> *"The truth told with ill intent beats*
> *all the lies you can invent"*
> *(William Blake, 1757-1827)*

4.  I promise to begin to cause no harm to myself or others, inside myself or outside myself, at any time or any place, for any reason, except to protect my loved ones and myself.
5.  I promise to begin to be happy most of the time; to get happy as soon as possible when I am unhappy, not at the expense of others; and to help others learn to be happy, if I can and they are ready to learn.
6.  I promise to feel the *healing feelings* over and over until they are automatically being felt most of the time and to feel them as quick as I can, except when I must protect my loved ones and/ or myself.

7. I promise to begin to keep my promises and to practice the ABCs of *healing feelings* with the *determination* of *zest* and *zeal*.

Signature_____ Date ___/___/_____

(Your signature is an honest commitment to all of yourself, conscious and unconscious, implicit and explicit to improve your life to the best of your ability.)


The ABCs of Healing Feelings; The Alphabet of Healing Feelings, aka;
The ABCs/Alphabet of Happiness/Happy/Healthy Feelings,
The ABCs/Alphabet of Wellbeing/Wellness/Wellerness/
Wholesomeness/Wholesome Feelings,
The ABCs/Alphabet of Self Esteem/Serenity/Peacefulness/
Positivity/Optimism/Contentment/Compassion,
Ronald L. Kelley, M.D., Distinguished Life Fellow
American Psychiatric Association
Copyright 2014

# ACKNOWLEDGMENTS

Ronald Lee Kelley was born on March 16, 1939—a few months before WWII—and was an only child until his brother, Samuel Keith Kelley, was born on December 26, 1957. Ronnie, his childhood name, was deeply influenced by his industrious middle-class parents and grandparents. Randal and Dollie Jones—on his mother's side—were tobacco farmers, and Br. Randal was also a lay Baptist preacher, who was Ronnie's first mentor. Rollie and Lucille Kelley—on his father's side—were farmers, and Rollie later became a successful small businessman and owned a successful chicken hatchery business. Rev. Robert Kelley, Rollie's father, was a farmer and a Methodist preacher.

Ronnie's father, Samuel Lee Kelley, was drafted when Ronnie just turned five years old. Sam, the name he was called, was stationed in Camp Blanding, Florida; Fort Meade, Maryland; Tule Lake, California; and Salt Lake City, Utah.

Christine loved to tell a story of their arrival in Tule Lake many times with tears in her eyes. The last part of their trip was by a bus full of military families. As the bus arrived at the outskirts, the bus driver slowed the bus down due to passing the barbed wire-surrounded camp. It so happened that Pfc. Sam Kelley was standing guard at the front gate. When Ronnie saw him, according to Christine, Ronnie started screaming "There's my daddy! There's my daddy! There's my daddy!" repeatedly. The bus driver began to laugh and stopped the bus to let Ronnie get off the bus and see his daddy.

The story further goes that Ronnie looked up to his daddy and said, "Daddy, you've got your gun!" Christine, with a tear in her eye each time she told this story, said, "There was not an eye on the bus without a tear."

Ronnie, by time he was six years old, had identified with being a preacher, a soldier, or an artist. Professor Boaz told him after his sculpture class he was the only art student who could sell his art.

He graduated from Murray High School in 1958 and was not in the upper third of his class. MHS was less than four hundred students, and the classes averaged thirty students. He played the trumpet and was in a Junior High marching band but could not make first chair in trumpet and quit to play football. He was a very aggressive linebacker and suffered a shoulder injury in his senior year. He was nick named "Shipwreck" by Haron West, his favorite coach. He was named because he always gave 110 percent when he played sports.

Christine, Ronnie's mother, became very concerned about Ronnie developing a habitual vocal tic. She consulted several MD's without success. A neighbor talked her into seeing a new chiropractor in town. Within two weeks, the psychosomatic vocal tic was gone. Dr. Abernathy became a friend of the family and circle of friends. He was an orphan at three and born in Kirksville, Missouri, the home of Osteopathic medicine. He originally aspired to become an osteopathic doctor. He was raised by very kind foster parents which accounted for his kindness. He married early, which ended his aspiration to become a DO. He had three daughters, no sons and a failed marriage. After military service, a successful business and a second failed marriage he decided to go to the San Antonio Chiropractic School. Why he came to the little college town of Murray, Kentucky is not known.

He became Ronnie's second mentor and taught the future Dr. Ron Kelley, MD, to become a healer. Ronnie first wanted to be a chiropractor but Dr. Abernathy, DC, wanted Ronnie to be an osteopath so he could do what both a medical doctor and a chiropractor could do. Dr. Abernathy performed many types of physical adjustments and hypnotic techniques on Ronnie, beginning when he was eight years old.

When Kelley, the name his high school peers called him, began to question his original religious beliefs, he became moody for several months. His loyal friends and girlfriend became concerned. One Sunday evening, he went with his girlfriend to her Methodist church.

After the sermon, he had to talk to Rev. Lyles and said, "I cannot believe all those people in India who have never heard the word Jesus are going to hell." Rev. Lyles looked at Kelley and said, "I don't either." He then gave Kelley a book to read on comparative religion and said, "You are thinking beyond your years." Kelley could not understand many of the new words and consequently read several vocabulary books until he could understand. This was the beginning of his self-education, for he became obsessed with understanding "The Truth!" It was only in his psychotherapy, during his psychiatric residence, that he developed the insight that he had identified with his maternal grandfather, who would sigh almost every day and say, "Know the truth and the truth will make you free" (John 8:32, KJV). Ron studied in depth several religious and metaphysical philosophies and eventually became a spiritual Christian.

At the age of sixteen, he read a book that Dr. Abernathy gave him. It was *The Introduction to Psychoanalysis* by Sigmund Freud, MD. It began to liberate Kelley to an open mind. Kelley then decided to become a psychiatrist, and especially, a psychoanalyst.

Ron, Kelley's adult name, went to Murray State College in his hometown, initially as a premed student, switched to majoring in history, was set up for a scholarship for a master's degree at Duke University, to be followed by a PhD in history at the University of Rochester. Ron turned it down to return to premed and go into debt to be a medical doctor. Dr. Frank Steeley, PhD, his history professor, never forgave him. Ron was on a drill team and was also a pledge master in the military fraternity of Perishing Rifles.

Sam and Christine owned the Kelley Pest Control Company, and he worked his way through college supporting his first wife, son, and himself by working for his father and consequently learning business skills. He graduated from MSU without debt, and after five years, he had majors in biology and history, and minors in philosophy, chemistry, and the advanced military science. (Reserved Officers Training Corps, ROTC.)

After graduation in 1963, Ron went for his medical evaluation to become a Second Lieutenant Infantry Officer and undoubtable deployment to Vietnam and almost certain physical and or mental injury or death. To his surprise, he was not combat qualified due to a football injury to his left shoulder. It was too late to apply to a medical school, so he taught high school chemistry in Kentland, a rural community in northwest Indiana, for one year. He and his first wife divorced during a separation that year. They remarried his junior year in medical school and had two more sons, and eventually divorced again.

Ron later married Molly Wilson, the love of his life, and he has two surviving sons, two stepdaughters that Molly and he raised, and are blessed with seven grandchildren together in the last thirty years.

Ron was accepted by the University of Louisville Medical School. All of his electives were in psychiatry, psychology, or neurology. Just before he graduated in 1968, an Army recruiter visited and informed his class that if a medical doctor did not volunteer for the military services, 95 percent would be drafted before the age of thirty-five years old, twenty-seven for all other males. Ronald Kelley, MD, Capt. MC, USA, had his rotating medical internship at William Beaumont US Army Hospital, Ft. Bliss near El Paso, Texas. He was the organizer and was the master of ceremonies of a three-part play, involving all of the twenty-seven interns who participated in roasting the medical staff at the end of their internship. He was accepted for a psychiatric residency at the Walter Reed US Army Medical Center, Washington, D.C.

"My most respected psychiatric teacher commented in his book, *Making Mistakes*, that all of us, since William the Conquer in 1066, have approximately 1.2 million ancestors. For some reason, that stuck in my mind. Ken Artist, MD, LtC. MC, USA Ret., was one of those "90-day wonders" in World War II who was transformed from a general medical officer, with a cram course, to be an infantry division psychiatrist in 90 days. He was one of those professors that others and I admired and hated at the same time. His undeclared endeavor was to make you a toughminded soldier and a smarter military psychiatrist. Not only were you expected to be a sensitive, dedicated medical doctor, pharmacotherapist, and psychodynamic psychiatrist, but also an administrator and social psychiatrist that was trained to understand, train, manage, and lead large groups of individuals.

"It took me some time to insightfully understand the origin of my ambivalence with this man. He wore a thin mustache similar to my second mentor, Dr. Abernathy, who unless he was treating you, had a friendly kind look in his large intense eyes. Dr. Artist's eyes were stern with a little bit of sadism. Perhaps it was due to his undoubted lifelong stuttering, which was noticeable but not severe enough to be completely impairing. I suspected he and his psychiatrist once examined his perhaps childhood ridicule related to his stuttering. He seemed to unintentionally enjoy the pain when one gained a harsh insight, while painfully losing an attachment to a false idea."

After completing a three-year of psychiatry and neurology residency, he was ordered to be chief of psychiatry at Ft. Campbell US Army Hospital, then after successfully reorganizing and improving the psychiatric department, he was ordered to be the Second Infantry Division psychiatrist on the demilitarized zone in the Republic of Korea, where he again reorganized and improved the psychiatric service in the Second Med. Bn., Second Inf. Div., Eighth US Army.

He had to decline an early promotion to lieutenant colonel and an assignment to a military teaching hospital. He had already declined an earlier offer to be a professor in the Vanderbilt Psychiatric Department. All of this was due to a contractual obligation to the state of Kentucky, to practice in a rural area for several years. This was a curse and a blessing for it kept Major Kelley from being eventually an administrator in the Army and a subspecialized professor in a university. Instead, he became a broadly experienced psychotherapist, medical doctor, and general psychiatrist. His most successful original contribution to many of his psychotherapy patients is his ego-building technique, *The ABCs of Healing Feelings*.

Dr. Kelley established a large psychiatric practice in Paducah, Kentucky, near his hometown of Murray, and has been active in teaching many mental health students as an assistant clinical professor of psychiatry of the University of Kentucky, teaching seminars and lectures, serving as the president of the Kentucky Medical Psychiatric Association, chief of staff for Lourdes Hospital, and other professional and civic activities.

He is still in private practice, teaching students, and is bossed around by Molly, his lovely wife of thirty years, and sometimes his grandchildren.

I am grateful for the many mentors and teachers in my life, but my best teachers have been my students, and especially, my myriad of patients.

I am thankful for the assistance of the following who have helped me in this endeavor:

Cindy Parrish, my publication assistant; Alexis Ari Arakelian, my first editor; Dr. Sam Kelley, MD, my brother; Judge Bill Graves, my attorney, advisor and friend; Richard "Dick" Flaherty, MSW, my friend since training at Walter Reed Medical Center; Dr. Anthony "Tony" Leskosky, MD, my neuroradiology friend; Dr. Elmer Maggard, PhD, my friend who is a clinical psychologist; R. Gordon Williams, PhD, a clinical psychologist with whom I have I have practices with for many years; Cindy Williams Bebout, my supportive office coordinator; and Molly Kelley BSW, my patient wife.

I am deeply grateful for my mentors (apart from my family) who have enriched my treasured education and unexpected experiences. I must mention one—my "Papaa," who has had a profound positive influence on me—shaping my core personhood; his daughter, Christine, my mother, who would have given the shirt off her back for my brother and my education; and my father, Sam, who taught me a work ethic, business skills, positive relationships and leadership.

Outside my biological family, "Dr. Bill" William Abernathy DO, renovated my body and soul, aspired me with the hope to become the healer that I am and his wife Elizabeth who dedicated her life to kindness and service to others, taught me the power of kindness.

Then Mildred Ragsdale, my playmates mother, who loved me like a mother and her daughter Faye, who taught me how to relate affectionately to women.

My coaches who taught me group cooperation: Haron West, who nicked named me "Shipwreck Kelley" and Dub Russel, who would often say, "Something is wrong with you, Kelley," due to my moody, questioning introspection.

Rev. Paul Lyles, my pastor and theology teacher, who told me I was "thinking beyond your age" and gave me a book to read on comparative religion.

My primary metaphysical teachers were Dr. Thurman Fleet, DC and Jack Inch of the Concept Therapy Institute, who taught me the beginning of spiritual discernment.

Later at Murray State University Professor Dr. Liza Spann, PhD was my admired premed advisor. Professor Robert Perkins was my illuminating philosophy instructor. Professor Bill Boaz, my friend and muse creator art teacher, who told me "You are the only one I know who can sell your art." Dr. Frank Seeley, PhD, my attentive history professor.

At the University of Louisville I owe the beginning of the shaping of my neuropsychiatric mind to: Dr. William Keller, MD, Chairman of the Department of Psychiatry who took a special interest in me and my close coed friend, Dr. Sandy Elam, MD (later a child psychiatrist); Dr. Clovis Crabtree, MD, previously a General Practitioner who taught me the beginning of clinical medicine and was my first supervising psychiatric resident; Dr. John Ice, MD, the Chief of Child Psychiatry, who taught me dream interpretation. Dr. Ephriam Roseman, MD the Chief of Neurology and an unforgettable challenging professor taught me the beginning of clinical neurology; and finally, Dr. Maynard, PhD, the intense professor of psychology under whom I enjoyed 18 elective credit hours in basic psychology on the University of Louisville Campus.

My psychiatric professors at the Walter Reed Medical Center Residency were: Bruce Bailey, MD, Col. MC, USA and Frank Jones, MD, Col. MC, USA, my psychiatric residence directors, guided me through an intense psychiatric residency program during the Vietnam War and taught me numerable valuable practical lessons. Important others were: Dr. Kenneth Artist, MD, LtC. MC, USA Ret., who taught via small group seminar discussions with selective germane intervention and management literature. They ranged from individual psychological phenomena and to large group, national and cultural behavior; William Stockton, MD, Col. MC, USA Ret., President of the Institute of the Philadelphia Association for Psychoanalysis, who taught me the continuous learning art of psychiatric interviewing; John Follonsbee, MD, LtC. MC, USA, my thoughtful psychoanalysis supervisor; Edward Nace, MD, Capt. MC, USA, my hypnosis research teacher; Dr. Morris Parloff, PhD, a WWII American Spy in Germany and later a brilliant researcher in individual and group psychotherapy at the National Institute of Mental Health, who supervised and taught my psychiatric co-resident Robert Lenox, MD, Capt. MC, USA, and me small group psychotherapy for two years; Harry Holloway, MD, Col. MC, USA, then Director of Neuropsychiatry at Walter Reed Army Institute of Research (the RAND Corporation of the Army), later the Chairman of the Department Psychiatry at the Uniform Services University Health Sciences (USUHS) and other national positions, a profoundly gifted genius, teacher and compassionate psychiatrist. It was serendipity that he was my milieu and ward management teacher and supervisor for two years.

*"We are not the whole of ourselves, those who*
*we have given our faith are the rest of us."*
*(Thurman Fleet, 1895-1983)*

# SOURCES

1   http://learnenglishkids.britishcouncil.org/songs/the-alphabet-song

2   Vico G, Danesi M. Metaphor and the Origin of Language Marcel Danesi September 22, 1993 Indiana University Press

3   Walter de Gruer. Approaches to Seminotics in Thomas A. Sebeok, Alexandra Ramsayok I, /Book B, Approaches to Animal Communication—Language Arts & Disciplines, p 72

4   Coll. Antripol.24(2000) 2: 541-553UDC 527.026<<Original scientific paper Symbolism in Prehistoric Man, F, Faccin p 541-553

5   Bodrova, E. & Leong, D.J. (1996) Tools of the Mind: The Vygotskian approach to early childhood education. Columbus: Merrill/Prentice Hall.

6   Morten Overgaard. The Status and Future of Consciousness Research. Front Psychol. 2017; 8: 1719. Published online 2017 Oct 10. doi: 10.3389/fpsyg.2017.01719 PMCID: PMC5641373 PMID: 29066988

7   Stanislas Dehaene, Lionel Naccache Unite. Towards a cognitive neuroscience of consciousness: basic evidence and a workspace framework ¬INSERM 334, Service Hospitalier Fre¬de¬ric Joliot, CEA/DRM/DSV, 4, Place du Ge¬ne¬ral Leclerc,91401 Orsay Cedex, France Received 8 February 2000; accepted 27 September 2000

8   NIMH » Construct: Perception https://www.nimh.nih.gov ›

9   NIMH » NIMH » ERP components—RDoC Element https://www.nimh.nih.gov › research › rdoc › units › physiology. The following construct(s)/subconstruct(s) refer to this element... Domain: Cognitive Systems · Construct: Perception ·

10  Pomerantz, James R. (2003): "Perception: Overview". In: Lynn Nadel (Ed.), Encyclopedia of Cognitive Science, Vol. 3, London: Nature Publishing Group, pp. 527–537.

11  Gibson, Eleanor J. Introductory Essay: What does infant perception tell us about theories of perception? Journal of Experimental Psychology: Human Perception and Performance, Vol 13(4), Nov 1987, 515-523

12  Debra Trampe, Jordi Quoidbach, Maxime Taquet Editor Emotions in Everyday Life. Avenanti, Editor Emotions in Everyday Life PLoS One. 2015; 10(12): e0145450. Published online 2015 Dec 23. doi: 10.1371/journal.pone.0145450 PMCID: PMC4689475

13  Phillips, Maggie. Empowering the Self Through Ego-State Therapy. Subscribe to email newsletter at www.maggiephillipsphd.com…

14  David Daniels, Terry Saracen, Meghan Fraley, Jennifer Christian, Seth Pardo. Advancing Ego Development in Adulthood Through Study of the Enneagram System of Personality. Journal of Adult Development, December 2018, Volume 25, Issue 4, pp 229–241

15  Jonathan St. B. T. Evans. Rationality and the illusion of choice Front. Psychol., 12 February 2014 | https://doi.org/10.3389/fpsyg.2014.00104

16  Mia Doring. Very Brief Introduction to Choice Theory. https://www.headstuff.org › Topical › Science › Psychology, https://www.youtube.com › Video for science of psychology of choice May 9, 2017 -

17  Martin E.P. Seligman | Positive Psychology Center, https://ppc.sas.upenn.edu › people › martin-ep-seligma

18  https://www.pursuit-of-happiness.org › barb-fredrickson

19  Nicholas Tarrier (2010). Broad Minded Affective Coping (BMAC): A "Positive" CBT Approach to Facilitating Positive Emotions. International Journal of Cognitive Therapy: Vol. 3, Special Section: Disgust and Psychopathology, pp. 64-76.

20  https://www.psychologytoday.com/us/blog/the-athletes-way/201507/the-neuroscience-savoring-positive-emotions

21  Aaron S. Heller, Andrew S. Fox, Erik K. Wing, Kaitlyn M. McQuisition, Nathan J. Vack and Richard J. Davidson. The Neurodynamics of Affect in the Laboratory Predicts Persistence of Real-World Emotional Responses. Journal of Neuroscience 22 July 2015, 35 (29) 10503-10509; DOI: https://doi.org/10.1523/JNEUROSCI.0569-15.2015

22  HM Sisti, TJ Shors. Neurogenesis and learning: Learning predicts how many new neurons survive.—fens2006.neurosciences.asso.fr

23  Gary T. Philips GT, Kopec AM, Carew TJ. Neurobiology of Learning and Memory. Pattern and predictability in memory formation: from molecular mechanisms to clinical relevance and predictability in memory formation: From molecular mechanisms to clinical relevance. https://doi.org/10.1016/j.nlm.2013.05.003.[HTML] nih.gov

24  Pavlick Jr. P, Bolster T, Koedinger SW, MacWhinney B. Using Optimally Selected Drill Practice to Train Basic Facts. International Conference on Intelligent Tutoring Systems. ITS 2008: Intelligent Tutoring Systems pp 593-602. Department of Psychology Carnegie Mellon University Pittsburgh. Part of the Lecture Notes in Computer Science book series (LNCS, volume 5091)

25  Kandel, ER, Schwartz, JH. Molecular biology of learning: modulation of transmitter release. Science 29 Oct 1982: Vol. 218, Issue 4571, pp. 433-443 DOI: 10.1126/science.6289442

26  Jennifer S. Learner, Dacher Keltner. Beyond valence: Toward a model of emotion-specific influences on judgement and choice. Cognition and Emotion, 2000,14(4), 473-493

27  Chester DS, DeWall CN, Enjaian B. Sadism and Aggressive Behavior: Inflicting Pain to Feel Pleasure. Pers Soc Psychol Bull. 2019 Aug;45(8):1252-1268. doi: 10.1177/0146167218816327. Epub 2018 Dec 20.

28  Baron, Robert A. Negative effects of destructive criticism: Impact on conflict, self-efficacy, and task performance. Journal of Applied Psychology, Vol 73(2), May 1988, 199-207

29  Michelle Nadine Servaas, Harriëtte Riese, Remco Renken, Bernard Cornelis Marsman, Johan Lambregs, Johan Ormel, and

André Aleman, Yu-Feng Zang, Editor. The Effect of Criticism on Functional Brain Connectivity and Associations with Neuroticism. PLoS One. 2013; 8(7): e69606. Published online 2013 Jul 26. doi: 10.1371/journal.pone.0069606. PMCID: PMC3724923. PMID: 23922755

30    Cohen, Josh. "The History and Evolution of The Major System for Memorizing Numbers". Art of Memory.

31    Bower, Gordon H. (September–October 1970). "Analysis of a Mnemonic Device: Modern psychology uncovers the powerful components of an ancient system for improving memory". American Scientist. 58 (5): 496–510.

32    Navimipour NJ, Soltant, Z. The impact of cost, technology acceptance and employees' satisfaction on the effectiveness of the electronic customer relationship management systems. Computers in Human Behavior, 2016—Elsevier

33    Vøllestad, MB Nielsen, GH Nielsen. Mindfulness-and acceptance-based interventions for anxiety disorders: A systematic review and meta-analysis. British journal of clinical psychology 51 (3), 239-260

34    J Vøllestad, MB Nielsen, GH Nielsen. Mindfulness-and acceptance-based interventions for anxiety disorders: A systematic review and meta-analysis. British journal of clinical psychology 51 (3), 239-260

35    Watkinson, John G. The affect bridge: A hypnoanalytic technique. International Society of Clinical and Experimental Hypnosis, Vol 19, 1971- Issue I, Pages 21-27, Published online: 31 Jan 2008. http://doi.org/10.1080/00207147148.

36    Ann M. Graybiel, Scott G. Grafton. The Striatum: Where Skills and Habits Meet. Cold Spring Harbor Perspectives in Biology. https://cshperspectives.cshlp.org/content/7/8/a021691.short

37 38    Margaret A. Chesney, Lynae A. Darbes, Kate Hoerste, Jonelle M. Taylor, Donald B. Chambers, David E. Anderson. Positive emotions: exploring the other hemisphere in behavioral medicine. June 2005, 12:50

39    Morten L. Kringelbach, D. Phil, and Kent C. Berridge, Ph.D. The Functional Neuroanatomy of Pleasure and Happiness. Discov

Med. 2010 June; 9(49): 579-587. PMCID; PMC3008353 NIHMSID: NIHMS257671 PMID

40    Gruber, Jane. The Oxford Handbook of Positive Emotion and Psychopathology. Oxford Press p 546, https://bookd.google.com>books. The Oxford Handbook of Positive Emotion and Psychopathology

41    Carla Cunha, Riccardo Brambilla, and Kerrie L. Thomas. A Simple Role for BDNF in Learning and Memory? Front Mol Neurosci. 2110; 3: 1. Published online 2010 Feb 9. Prepublished online 2009 Oct 8. doi: 10.3389/neuro.02.001.2110

42    Fava Ga, Rafanelli C, Cazzaro M, Conti S, Grandi S. Well-being therapy. A novel psychotherapeutic approach for residual symptoms of affective disorders. Psychologic

43    https://en.wiktionary.org/wiki/acceptance

44    https://en.wikipedia.org/wiki/Acceptance

45    Heatherton, Todd F. Neuroscience of Self and Self-Regulation. Annu Rev Psychol. 2011; 62: 363-390. doi: 10.1146/annurev.psych. 121208.131616

46    Kelley WM, Macrae CN, Wyland CL, Caglar, S, Inzti S, Heatherton TF, Finding the self? An event-related fMRI study. J Cogn Ndurosci. 2002 Jul 1;14(5):785-944

47    Northhoff G, Heinzel A, de Gredk M, Bermpohl F, Dobrowollny H, Panksepp. Self-referential processing in our brain—a meta-analysis of imaging studies on the self. Neuroimage. 2006 May 15:31 (1):440-57. 2006 Fw 7.

48    Georg Northoff, Pengmin Qin & Todd E. Feinberg—2011 Brain Imaging of the Self-Conceptual, Anatomical and Methodological Issues.—*Consciousness and Cognition* 20 (1):52-63.

49    John T. Cacioppo, Gary G. Berntson, Jean Decety. Social Neuroscience and Its Relationship to Social Psychology. Cogn. 2010, 28(6). 675-685.

50    Laurita, Anne C. An attachment theoretical perspective for the neural representation of close others. Social Cognitive and Affective Neuroscience, Volume 14, Issue 3, March 2019, Pages 237–251.

51    Decety, Jean, Chaminade, Thierry. When the self represents the other: A new cognitive neuroscience view on psychologi-

cal identification. Social Cognitive Neuroscience, Center for Mind, Brain and Learning, University of Washington, Seattle, WA 98195, USA Received 27 February 003 Consciousness and Cognition 12 (2003) 5777-596

52    Lucia Francesca Menna. The scientific approach to Pet Therapy The Method and Training according to the Federiciano Model Lucia Francesca Menna Copyright © 2018—University of Naples Federico II Department of Veterinary Medicine and Animal Production, University of Naples Federico II Via Mezzocannone, 8- Naples

53    Yorke, Jan. Pages 559-570 | Received 23 Jan 2008, Accepted 29 Apr 2008, Published online: 12 Jun 2008. https://doi. org/10.1080/03004430802181189. The significance of human–animal relationships as modulators of trauma effects in children: a developmental neurobiological perspective. Journal Early Child Development and Care. Volume 180, 2110. Issue 5. Pages 559-570 | Received 23 Jan 2008, Accepted 29 Apr 2008, Published online: 12 Jun 2008

54    Sandra McCune, Katherine A. Kruger, James A. Griffin, Layla Esposito, Lisa S. Freund, Karyl J. Hurley, Regina Bures. Evolution of research into the mutual benefits of human–animal interaction. Sandra McCune, Katherine A. Kruger, Animal Frontiers, Volume 4, Issue 3, July 2014, Pages 49–58, Published: 01 July 2014

55    Wheeler MA, Stuss DT, Tulving EP. Toward a theory of episodic memory: the frontal lobes and autonoetic.sychol Bull. 1997 May. 121(3):331-Rotman Research Institute of Baycrest Centre, Toronto, Ontario, Canada. PPmarkw@psych.toronto.edu

56    Philip Corlett & Nataza Marrouch. social cognitive neuroscience of attitudes and beliefs. in Handbook of Attitudes. Edition: 2. Publisher: Routledge. Editors: Dolores Albarracin, Blair. T Johnson. Dec 27, 2018—P

57    Heller, A., Fox, A., Wing, E., McQuisition, K., Vack, N., & Davidson, R. (2015). The Neurodynamics of Affect in the Laboratory Predicts Persistence of Real-World Emotional Responses Journal of Neuroscience, 35 (29), 10503-10509 DOI: 10.1523/JNEUROSCI.0569-15.2015

58 Madan CR, Scott SME, Kinsingerr EA. Positive emotion enhances association-memory. Emotion. 2019 Jun;19(4):733-740. doi: 10.1037/emo0000465. Epub 2018 Aug 20.

59 Barron HC. Vogels TF, Brhrens TB, Ramaswami, M. Inhibitory engrams in perception and memory. Proc Natl Acad Sci U S A. 2017 Jun 27; 114(26): 6666–6674. Published online 2017 Jun 13. doi: 10.1073/pnas.1701812114 Neuroscience

60 Benedek M, Schües T, Beaty RE, Jauka E, Koschutnig K, Fink A, Neubauer AC. To create or to recall original ideas: Brain processes associated with the imagination of novel object uses. Cortex. Author manuscript; available in PMC 2018 Feb 7. Published in final edited form as: Cortex. 2018 Feb; 99: 93–102. Published online 2017 Nov 11. doi: 10.1016/j.cortex.2017.10.024

61 Mayseless N, Eran A, Shamay-Tsoory SG. Generating original ideas: The neural underpinning of originality. Neuroimage. 2015 Aug 1;116:232-9. doi: 10.1016/j.neuroimage.2015.05.030. Epub 2015 May 1047. 20.

62 Guan, F, Xiang Y, Chen o, Wang W, Chen J. Neural Basis of Dispositional Awe. Front. Behav. Neurosci., 11 September 2018 | https://doi.org/10.3389/fnbeh.2018.00209

63 Bevilacqua L, Goldman D. Genetics of emotion. Trends Cogn Sci. Author manuscript; available in PMC 2012 Sep 1. Published in final edited form as: Trends Cogn Sci. 2011 Sep; 15(9): 401–408. Published online 2011 Aug 10. doi: 10.1016/j.tics.2011.07.009

64 Tal E. Measurement in Science (Stanford Encyclopedia of Philosophy)http://plato.standford.edu>entries>measure-ment-science 2015

65 Yanaqisawa K, Abe N, Kashima ES, Nomura M. Self-esteem modulates amygdala-ventrolateral prefrontal cortex connectivity in response to mortality threats. J Exp Psychological Gen. 2016 Mar. 145(3):273-83. doi: 10.1037/xge0000121. Epub 1015 Nov 16

66 Rolls ET. A Biased Activation Theory of the Cognition and Attentional Modulation of Emotion. Front Hum Neurosci. 2013 Mar 18;7:74. doi: 10.3389/fnhum.2013.00074. eCollection 2013

67 Wathan J, Burrows AM, Waller BM, McComb K (2015) Correction: EquiFACS: The Equine Facial Action Coding System. PLOS ONE 10(9): e0137818. 3 Sep 2015

68 Sankey C, Richard-Yriss, M-A, LeRoy H, Henry S, Hausberger M. Positive interactions lead to lasting positive memories in horses, Equus caballus Animal Behavior. Vol 79, Isue 4, April 2010, p 869-875

69 Welsh PC. The Project Gutenberg EBook of Woodworking Tools 1600-1900, Woodworking Tools 1600-1900. November 12, 2008 [EBook #27238] www.gutenberg.net

70 Susman RL, Stern JT. Morphology of Homo habilis. Science. 1982 Sep 3;217(4563):931-4.

71 Marzke MW. Tool making, hand morphology and fossil hominins, Philos Trans R Soc Lond B Biol Sci. 2013 Nov 19; 368(1630): 20120414. doi: 10.1098/rstb.2012.0414

72 Marzke MW. Tool making, hand morphology and fossil hominins. Philos Trans R Soc Lond B Biol Sci. 13 Nov 19; 368(1630): 20120414. soi: 10.1098/rstb.2012.0414

73 Emotional security-Wikipedia. https://wikapedia.org/wikapedia/Emotional_security

74 Cherland E. The Polyvagal Theory: Neurophysiological Foundations of Emotions, Attachment, Communication, Self-Regulation. J Can Acad Child Adolesc Psychiatry. 2012 Nov; 21(4): 313–314. PMCID: PMC3490536

75 Edmons RA, McNamara P. Sacred Emituibs and Neurosxience. Robert A. Emmons and Patrick McNamara. Sacred Emotions and. Affective Neuroscience: Gratitude, Costly Signaling, and the Brain. 2006. polatulat.narod.ru>dvc>com.sacred_emotions

76 Vallant GE. Positive Emotions, Spirituality and the Practice of Psychiatry in George E. Vaillant, Mens Sana Monogr. 2008 Jan-Dec; 6(1): 48–62. 10.4103/0973-1229.36504 \\PMCID: PMC3190563.: 22013350

77 Zaaccaro A, Plartyyi A, Lariuno M, Garbrlla E, Menicucci D, Neri B, Germignani A. How Breath-Control Can Change Your Life: A Systematic Review on Psycho-Physiological Correlates of Slow Breathing. Fron/ Hum. Neurosci., 07 September 2018.

Front. Hum. Neurosci., 07 September 2018 |. https://doi.org/10.3389/fnhum.2018.00353

78 Gerberg p. Brown R. Neurobiology and Neurophysiology of Breath Care. Psychiatric Times, Vol 33 Issue 11. November 30, 2016

79 Meinychuk MC, Dockree RM, O'Connell RG, Murphy PR, Baisters JH, Robertson IH. Coupling of respiration and attention via the locus coeruleus: Effects of meditation and pranayama. Psychophysiology 8-2010 December 2019 Heidleberg, Germany Vol 55, Issue 0 September 2018. First published: 22 April 2018 http://dol.org/10.1111/psyp.13091

80 Crane M. Should doctors be prescribing cats? The Refresh Comment. www.therefresh.co › 2017/07/20

81 Qureshi A, Memon MZ, Vazquez G, Suri MF. Cat ownership and the Risk of Fatal Cardiovascular Diseases. Results from the Second National Health and Nutrition Examination Study Mortality Follow-up Study. J Vasc Interv Neurol. 2009 Jan; 2(1): 132-135. PMCID: PMC3317329 PMID: 2251840

82 von Muggenthaler E. The felid purr: A healing mechanism? The Journal of the Acoustical Society of America 110, 2666 (2001); https://doi.org/10.1121/1.4777098

83 Viero C, Shibuya I, Kitamura N, Verkhrat A, Fugihara H, Katoh A, Ueta Y, Zingg HH, Civatal A, Sykova E, Dayanathi G. KREVIEW: Oxytocin: Crossing the Bridge between Basic Science and Pharmacotherapy. CNS Neurosci Ther. 2010 Oct; 16(5): e138–e156. Published online 2010 Jul 7. doi: 10.1111/j.1755-5949.2010.00185.x PMCID: PMC2972642 PMID: 20626426

84 Jeon H, Lee S-H. From Neurons to Social Beings: Short Review of the Mirror Neuron System Research and Its Socio-Psychological and Psychiatric Implications. Clin Psychopharmacol Neurosci. 2018 Feb; 16(1): 18–31. Published online 2018 Feb 28. doi: PMCID: PMC5810456 PMID: 29397663

85 Lally P, van Jaarsveld, Potts HW, Wardle J. How Habits Are Formed: habit formation in the real world. European Journal of. Social Psychology.! 6bJuly 2009. https://doi.org/10.1002/ejsp.674

[86] Dolcos, S., Moore, M., & Katsumi, Y. (2018). Neuroscience and well-being. In E. Diener, S. Oishi, & L. Tay (Eds.), Handbook of well-being. Salt Lake City, UT: DEF Publishers. DOI: nob

[87] Alegre, A. (2008). "Emotional security and its relationship with emotional intelligence" (PDF). Virginia Polytechnic Institute and State University. Archived from the original (PDF) on 16 January 2014. Retrieved 21 November 2012.

[88] Maslow, A. H. (1942). "The Dynamics of Psychological Security-Insecurity". Journal of Personality. 10 (4): 331–344. doi:10.1111/j.1467-6494.1942.tb01911.x.

[89] Velikova S, Sjaaheim H, Nortug B. Can the Psycho-Emotional State be Optimized by Regular Use of Positive Imagery? Psychological and Electroencephalographic Study of Self-Guided Training. Frontiers in Human Neuroscience, 2017; 10 DOI: 10.3389/fnhum.2016.00664

[90] Murphy S, O'Donoghue MC, Drazich EHS, Blackwell SE, Nobre AC, Homes EH. Imagining a brighter future: The effect of positive imagery training on mood, prospective mental imagery and emotional bias in older adults. Psychiatry Res. 10.1016/j.psychres.2015.07.059 CPMCID: PMC4593863PMID:26235478

[91] Blackwell, S. E. Mental imagery: from basic research to clinical practice. Journal of Psychotherapy Integration. doi: 10.1037/int0000108. Journal of Psychotherapy Integration, Vol 29(3), Sep 2019, 235-247

[92] https://en.wiktionary.org/wiki/belonging

[93] Jeon H. From Neurons to Social Beings: Short Review of the Mirror Neuron System Research and Its Socio-Psychological and Psychiatric Implications. Clin Psychopharmacol Neurosci. 2018 Feb; 16(1): https://www.ncbi.nlm.nih.gov › pmc › articles › PMC5810456

[94] May, Vanessa. Belonging from afar: nostalgia, time and memory. The Sociological Review. 2017, Vol. 65 (2) 401-415 DOI: 10.1111/1467-954X.12402 journals.sagepub.com/home/sor

[95] Belongingness Wikipedia, the free encyclopedia. https://en.wikipedia.org/wiki/Belongingness#cite_note-Cockshaw-30

96   Emmons RA, McCullough ME. Counting Blessings Versus Burdens: An Experimental Investigation of Gratitude and Subjective Well-Being in Daily Life. J Personality and Social Psychology 2003, Vol. 84, No. 3, 377-398

97   Cela-Conde CJ (1), García-Prieto J, Ramasco JJ, Mirasso CR, Bajo R, Munar E, Flexas A, del-Pozo F, Maestú F. Dynamics of brain networks in the aesthetic appreciation. Proc Natl Acad Sci U S A. 2013 Jun 18;110 Suppl 2:10454-61. doi: 10.1073/pnas.1302855110. Epub 2013 Jun 10

98   Pearce MT, Zaidel DW, Vartanian O, Skov M, Leder H, Chatterjee A, Nadal M. Neuroaesthetics: The Cognitive Neuroscience of Aesthetic Experience Perspectives on Psychological Science 2016, Vol. 11(2) 265–279. DOI: 10.1177/1745691615621274 pps.sagepub.com

99   https://en.wiktionary.org/wiki/caring

100  Ashar et al. Empathic Care and Distress: Predictive Brain Markers and Dissociable Brain Systems, Neuron (2017), http://dx.doi.org/10.1016/j.neuron.2017.05.014Ashar et al., Empathic Care and Distress: Predictive Brain Markers and Dissociable Brain Systems, Neuron (2017), http://dx.doi.org/10.1016/j.neuron.2017.05.014

101  https://en.wiktionary.org/wiki/contentment

102  https://en.wikipedia.org › wiki › Contentment

103  https://en.wiktionary.org/wiki/compassion

104  https://en.wikipedia.org/wiki/Compassion

105  Klimecki OM, Leiberg S, Lamm C. Functional Neural Plasticity and Associated Changes in Positive Affect After Compassion Training Olga M. Klimecki, Susanne Leiberg, Claus Lamm, Tania Singer. Cerebral Cortex, Volume 23, Issue 7, July 2013, Pages 1552–1561

106  Leiberg, Susanne; Klimecki, Olga; Singer, Tania. Short-term compassion training increases prosocial behavior in a newly developed prosocial game DOI: or Website Link: 10.1371/journal.pone.99177982011LL

107  Jarlstrom, T. Neural Effects of Compassion Training for bachelor's degree Project in Cognitive Neuroscience Basic level

22.5 ECTS Spring term 2018 Toni Järlström Supervisor: Petri Kajonius Examiner: Stefan Berglund. University of Skovde, Sweden.

[108] https://en.wiktionary.org/wiki/cherishing

[109] https://en.wiktionary.org/wiki/caress

[110] https://en.wiktionary.org/wiki/curiosity

[111] https://en.wikipedia.org/wiki/Curiosity

[112] Celeste Kidd, Benjamin Y. Hayden The psychology and neuroscience of curiosity. Neuron. 2015 Nov 4; 88(3): 449–460. 10.1016/j.neuron.2015.09.010. PMCID: PMC4635443 NIHMSID: NIHMS722442 PMID: 26539887

[113] https://en.wiktionary.org/wiki/deserving

[114] Freeman DMC. The Contribution of Faith and Ego Strength to the Prediction of GPA among High School Students. Dissertation Submitted to the Faculty of the Virginia Polytechnic Institute and State University in partial fulfillment of the requirement for the degree of Doctorate of Philosophy I Human Development. https://vtechworks.lib.vt.edu/bitstream/handle/10919/26024/Dissertation..pdf?sequence=1. 18 December 2001

[115] https://en.wiktionary.org/wiki/desire

[116] https://en.wiktionary.org/wiki/happiness

[117] https://en.wikipedia.org/wiki/Happiness

[118] Morten L. Kringelbach and Kent C. Berridge. The Neuroscience of Happiness and Pleasure. Soc Res (New York). 2010 SUMMER; 77(2): 659–678. PMCID: PMC3008658 NIHMSID:NIHMS257673 PMID: 22068342

[119] https://en.wikipedia.org/wiki/Self-actualization

[120] Ng B. The Neuroscience of Growth Mindset and Intrinsic Motivation. Brain Sci. 2018 Jan 26;8(2). pii: E20. doi: 10.3390/brainsci8020020. Review. PMID: 29373496 Sci. 2018 Jan Sci. 2018 Jan 26;8(2). pii: E20. doi: 10.3390/brainsci8020020. Review.

[121] https://en.wiktionary.org/wiki/dedicate

[122] https://en.wikipedia.org/wiki/Dedication

[123] https://en.wiktionary.org/wiki/devotion

[124] https://en.wikipedia.org/wiki/Devotion

[125] https://en.wiktionary.org/wiki/divine

126   https://en.wikipedia.org/wiki/Divinity

127   Newberg AB. The neuroscientific study of spiritual practices. Front. Psychol., 18 March 2014 https://doi.org/10.3389/fpsyg.2014.00215

128   https://en.wiktionary.org/wiki/enjoyment

129   Berridge K. Simple Pleasures, New findings in hedonic psychology and affective neuroscience are revealing intriguing complexities. Psychological Science Agenda | November 2004.https://www.apa.org/science/about/psa/2004/11/berridge

130   https://web.archive.org/web/20121230030647/ http://www.umcmission.org/Find-Resources/Global-Worship-and-Spiritual-Growth/John-Wesley-Sermons/Sermon-37-The-Nature-of-Enthusiasm

131   https://dictionary.cambridge.org/us/dictioonary/dictionary/english/enthusiasm

132   https://en.wikipedia.org/wiki/Enthusiasm

133   https://en.wiktionary.org/wiki/enhance

134   https://en.wiktionary.org/wiki/enduring

135   https://en.wikipedia.org/wiki/Endurance

136   https://en.wiktionary.org/wiki/endearing

137   https://en.wiktionary.org/wiki/forgiveness

138   https://en.wikipedia.org/wiki/Talk:Forgiveness

139   https://en.wiktionary.org/wiki/faith

140   https://en.wikipedia.org/wiki/Faith

141   https://www.nimh.nih.gov/health/statistics/post-traumatic-stress-disorder-ptsd.shtml

142   Ricciardi E, Rota R, Sani Lk, Gentili C, Gaglianese A, Gjazzelk M, Pietrini P. How the Brain Heals Emotions: The Functional Neuroanatomy of Forgiveness. Font Hum Neurosci. 2013; 7: 839. Published online 2013 Dec 9. doi: 10.3389/fnhum.2013.00839 PMCID: 3856773 PMID: 24367315

143   Nu E. The Neurological Basis for Belief. in Science Summer 2011 Essay Competition, Second Place Essay. August 2011 Science. cis.org.uk.

144   The fascinating source of the word "fascinating." en.antiquitem.com Nov 5, 2013

145 https://en.wiktionary.org/wiki/fascinate

146 Filevidch E, Vqnn PM, Fia W, Haggard P, Kuhn Sl. Brain correlates of subjective freedom of choice. Consciousness and Cognition. Vol 22. Issue 4, Dec 2012, p 1271—https://doi. org/10.1016/j.concog.2013.08.011

147 https://en.wiktionary.org/wiki/goodness

148 https://en.wikipedia.org/wiki/Greater_Good_Science_Center

149 https://en.wiktionary.org/wiki/gratitude

150 https://en.wikipedia.org/wiki/Gratitude

151 Fox G, Kaplan J, Damasio H, Damasio TA. Neural correlates of gratitude. Front Psychol. 2015; 6: 1491.Published online 2015 Sep 30. doi: 10.3389/fpsyg.2015.01491 PMCID: PMC4588123 PMID: 26483740

152 https://en.wiktionary.org/wiki/grace

153 https://en.wikipedia.org/wiki/Divine_grace

154 https://en.wiktionary.org/wiki/hope

155 https://en.wikipedia.org/wiki/Hope

156 Rajandram RK, Ho SM, Samman N, Chan N, McGrath C, Swahlen R. Interaction of hope and optimism with anxiety and depression in a specific group of cancer survivors: a preliminary study. MC Res Notes. 2011; 4: 519. Published online 2011 Nov 28. doi: 10.1186/1756-0500-4-519 PMCID: PMC3314421 PMID: 22123081

157 https://en.wiktionary.org/wiki/humility

158 https://en.wikipedia.org/wiki/Humility

159 Amir O, Bierderman I. The Neural Correlates of Humor Creativity. Front Hum Neurosci. 2016; 10: 597. Published online 2016 Nov 25. doi: 10.3389/fnhum.2016.00597 PMCID: PMC5122582 PMID: 27932965

160 Vlachopoulos, C; Xaplanteris, P; Alexopoulos, N; Aznaouridis, K; Vasiliadou, C; Baou, K; Stefanadi, E; Stefanadis, C (2009). "Divergent effects of laughter and mental stress on arterial stiffness and central hemodynamics". Psychosom. Med. 71 (4): 446-53. Doi:10.1097/PSY. 0b01318198dcd4. PMID 19251872.

161 https://en.wikipedia.org/wiki/Laughter

[162] Williams PB. Your Brain on Happiness: The Neuroscience of Joy. truehomewithin.net>essay_joy10_brain_on_happiness2

[163] https://www.coursera.org/learn/the-science-of-well-being

[164] https://www.authentichappiness.sas.upenn.edu/home

[165] https://www.pursuit-of-happiness.org/history-of-happiness/barb-fredrickson/

[166] https://en.wikipedia.org/wiki/Special:Search?search=spiritual+heart&go=Go&n

[167] Rao A, Sibbritt D, Phillips JL, Hickman LD. Prayer or spiritual healing as adjuncts to conventional care: a cross sectional analysis of prevalence and characteristics of use among women. https://bmjoprn.com>content

[168] https://en.wiktionary.org/wiki/intelligence

[169] https://en.wikipedia.org/wiki/Intelligence

[170] Santarecchi E, Rossi S. Advances in the Neuroscience of Intelligence: from Brain Connectivity to Brain Perturbation. The Spanish Journal of Psychology (2016), 19, e94, 1–7. © Universidad Complutense de Madrid and Colegio Oficial de Psicólogos de Madrid doi:10.1017/sjp.2016.89

[171] Voltz KG, von Cramon DY. What neuroscience can tell about intuitive processes in the context of perceptual discovery. J Cogn Neurosci. 2006 Dec;18(12):2077-87

[172] Sadler-Smith SR. Intuition, neuroscience, Decision Making and Learning. Center for Management, Decision Making and Development, School of Management. September 2006. Triarchy Press ~ www.triarchypress.com. citeseerx.ist.psu.edu > viewdoc > download

[173] Kiteaayama S, Park J. Cultural neuroscience of the self: understanding the social grounding of the brain. Soc Cogn Affect Neurosci. 2010 Jun-Sep; 5(2-3): 111–129. Published online 2010 Jun 26. doi: 10.1093/scan/nsq052 PMCID: PMC2894676 PMID: 20592042

[174] D'Agembrau A, Casspl H. Phillips C, Balteau E, Salmon E, Der Linden MV. Brains creating stories of selves: the neural basis of autobiographical reasoning. Soc Cogn Affect Neurosci. 2014 May; 9(5): 646–652. Published online 2013 Mar 22.

doi: 10.1093/scan/nst028 PMCID: PMC4014101PMID: 23482628

175 Lirberman MB. Intuition: A Social Cognitive Neuroscience Approach. Psychological Bulletin Copyright 2000 by the American Psychological Association, Inc. 2000, Vol. 126, No. 1, 109-137 0033-2909/00/$5.00 DOI: 10.1037//0033-2909.126.1.109

176 Agnati LF, Guiodlin D, Battistin L, Pagnoni G, Fuxe K. The Neurobiology of Imagination: Possible Role of Interaction-Dominant Dynamics and Default Mode Network. Front Psychol. 2013; 4: 296.Published online 2013 May 24. doi: 10.3389/fpsyg.2013.00296 PMCID: PMC3662866 PMID: 23745117

177 https://en.wiktionary.org/wiki/fantasy

178 https://en.wikipedia.org/wiki/Fantasy

179 https://en.wikipedia.org/wiki/Fantasy_(psychology)

180 Macing, D. Different Uses of Fantasy in Working with Images. Conference, Symposia and Events. Edith Cowan University Research Online. INSCAPE—ARTCAP November 13-16, 2003 *https://pdfs.semanticscholar.org*

181 https://www.goodreads.com/author/show/3527279. August_Kekul_

182 Barrett D. Dreams and creative problem-solving. Annaks of the New York Academy if /sciences. 22 June 2017. https://doi.org/10.1111/nyas13412

183 https://en.wiktionary.org/wiki/joy

184 https://en.wikipedia.org/wiki/Joy

185 Ungar T. Neuroscience, Joy, and the Well-Infant Visit That Got Me Thinking. Ann Fam Med January/February 2017 vol. 15 no. 1 80-83 doi: 10.1370/afm.2013 Ann Fam Med January/February 2017 vol. 15 no. 1 80-83

186 Barak Y. The immune system and happiness. Autoimmun Rev. 2006 Oct:5(8):523-7. Epub 2006 Mar 21 ttps://www.ncbi.nlm.nih.gov/pubmed/17027886#

187 Bryant FB, Smart CM, King SP. Using the Past to Enhance the Present: Boosting Happiness Through Positive Reminiscence. Journal of Happiness Studies. September 2005, Volume 6, Issue 3, pp 227–260

[188] Kimberly M. Livingstone, Srivastava S. Up-regulating positive emotions in everyday life: Strategies, individual differences, and associations with positive emotion and well-being. Journal of Research in Personality 46 (2012) 504–516 journal homepage: www.elsevier.com/locate/jrp

[189] https://en.wikisource.org/wiki/Eternity_(Blake)

[190] https://en.wiktionary.org/wiki/kindness

[191] https://en.wikipedia.org/wiki/Kindness

[192] Mathers N. Compassion and the science of kindness: Harvard Davis Lecture 2015. British Journal of General Practice 2016; 66 (648): e525-e527. DOI: https://doi.org/10.3399/bjgp16X686041

[193] Hofman SG, Grossma P, Hinton SE. Loving-Kindness and Compassion Meditation: Potential for Psychological Interventions. Clin Psychol Rev. 2011 Nov; 31(7): 1126–1132. 10.1016/j.cpr.2011.07.003Published online 2011 Jul 26. doi: PMCID: MC3176989NIHMSID: NIHMS315166 PMID: 218402891840289

[194] https://en.wiktionary.org/wiki/love

[195] https://en.wikipedia.org/wiki/Love

[196] Zeki S. 2019 The neurobiology of love. Federation of European Biochemical Societies. FEBS LettersVolume 581, Issue 14. Minireview. First published: 08 May 2007. https://doi.org/10.1016/j.febslet.2007.03.094

[197] https://en.wiktionary.org/wiki/loyal

[198] https://en.wikipedia.org/wiki/Loyalty

[199] https://en.wiktionary.org/wiki/compassion

[200] https://en.wikipedia.org/wiki/Compassion

[201] Esch T, Stefano GB. The neurobiological link between compassion and love. Med Sci Monit. 2011; 17(3): RA65–RA75. Published online 2011 Mar 1. doi: 10.12659/MSM.881441 PMCID: PMC3524717 PMID: 21358615

[202] https://en.wiktionary.org/wiki/agape

[203] https://en.wikipedia.org/wiki/Agape

[204] Cornwell J. The neuroscience of love, mysticism and poetry. Brain, Volume 132, Issue 11, November 2009, Pages 3187–

3190, https://doi.org/10.1093/brain/awp180. Published: 08 September 2009

205    Beauregard M, Courtemanche J, Paquette V, St-Pierre EL. The neural basis of unconditional love. Psychiatry Research: Neuroimaging 172 (2009) 93–98 Contents lists available at ScienceDirect Psychiatry Research: Neuroimaging journal homepage: www.elsevier.com/locate/psychresns

206    Ashar YK, Andrews-Hanna JR, Dimidjian S. Toward a Neuroscience of Compassion, Chapter (PDF Available) · June 2016 with 535 Reads DOI: 10.1093/acprof:oso/97801999779 25.003.0009In book: Positive Neuroscience, pp.125-142

207    https://en.wiktionary.org/wiki/longing

208    Most C. Maternal Infant Eye-To-Ey3 Gaze: Human Uniqueness Compared to "Great Apes": Relative Difference. Center for Academic Research & Training in Anthropogeny.https://carta. anthropogeny.org/moca/topics/maternal-infant-eye-eye-gaze, https://www.sciencedaily.com › releases › 2017/11

209    Simpson EH, Balsam PD. The Behavioral Neuroscience of Motivation: An Overview of Concepts, Measures, and Translational Applications. Curr Top Behav Neurosci. Author manuscript; available in PMC 2016 Dec 1. Published in final edited form as: Curr Top Behav Neurosci. 2016; 27: 1–12. doi: 10.1007/7854_2015_40

210    Heaterton TF. Neuroscience of Self and Self-Regulation. Annu Rev Psychol. Author manuscript; available in PMC 2011 Mar 14. Published in final edited form as: Annu Rev Psychol. 2011; 62: 363–390. doi: 10.1146/annurev.psych.121208.131616 PMCID: PMC3056504 NIHMSID: NIHMS245639 PMID: 21126181

211    Blattner T. The Neuroscience of Your Purpose and Personal Mission. https://medium.com>the neuroscience-of-your-per-sonal-mission... Jul 24, 2018

212    Marshall PJ, Meltzoff AN. Neuroimaging and mirroring in human infants. Philos Trans R Soc Lond B Biol Sci. 2014 Jun 5; 369(1644): 20130620. doi: 10.1098/rstb.2013.0620

213 Jeon H, Lee S-H. From Neurons to Social Beings: Short Review of the Mirror Neuron System Research and Its Socio-Psychological and Psychiatric Implications. Clin Psychopharmacol Neurosci. 2018 Feb; 16(1): 18–31. Published online 2018 Feb 28. doi: 10.9758/cpn.2018.16.1.18 PMCID: PMC5810456 PMID: 29397663

214 Turjman O. On the Role of Mirror Neurons in the Sense of Self. Semantic Scholar, ResearchGate PDF April 3016. https://pdfs.semanticscolar.org

215 Cascio CN, O'Donnell MB, Tinney FJ, Lieberman MD, Taylor SE, Strechr VJ, Falk EB. Self-affirmation activates brain systems associated with self-related processing and reward and is reinforced by future orientation. Published online 2015 Nov 5. doi: 10.1093/scan/nsv136 PMCID: PMC4814782 PMID: 26541373

216 https://en.wiktionary.org/wiki/notion

217 https://en.wikipedia.org/wiki/Notion_(philosophy)

218 Frederickson BL. The Role of Positive Emotions in Positive Psychology. Published in final edited form as: Am Psychol. 2001 Mar; 56(3): 218–226. PMCID: PMC3122271NIHMSID: NIHMS305177 PMID: 11315248

219 https://en.wikipedia.org/wiki/Open-mindedness

220 Lord ML. Group learning capacity: the roles of open-mindedness and shared vision. Front Psychol. 2015; 6: 150. Published online 2015 Feb 27. doi: 10.3389/fpsyg.2015.00150 PMCID: PMC4342883 PMID: 25774141

221 Lazar L. The Cognitive Neuroscience of Design Creativity. Exp Neurosci. 2018; 12: 1179069518809664. Published online 2018 Oct 31. doi: 10.1177/1179069518809664 PMCID: PMC6236478 PMID: 30450006

222 https://en.wikipedia.org/wiki/Intellectual_opportunism

223 Kennedy MB. Synaptic Signaling in Learning and Memory. Cold Spring Harb Perspect Biol. 2016 Feb; 8(2): a016824. doi: 10.1101/cshperspect.a016824 PMCID: PMC4743082 PMID: 24379319

224 https://en.wiktionary.org/wiki/wholesome

225 https://en.wiktionary.org/wiki/contentment, https://en.wikipedia.org/wiki/Contentment

226 https://en.wikipedia.org/wiki/Contentment

227 Gao Y. Edelson S. Between Pleasure and Contentment: Evolutionary Dynamics of Some Possible Parameters of Happiness. Plus One, Cognitive Neuroscience Channel. https://doi.org/10.1371/journal.pone.01553193

228 https://en.wikipedia.org/wiki/Emotion

229 Karlin B. The Simplicity of Stillness Method. Watkins Media Ltd; Release Date: December 3, 2015; Imprint: Watkins Publishing; ISBN: 9781780287553

230 Mendius R. Train Your Brain from Anger to Peace. Published on 12/11/07 (c) Rick Mendius, MD, 2008. https://rickkhanson.net>train-brain-anger-peace Mar 16, 2019

231 Yu C-H, Li L. Systems Neuroscience. Ann N Y Acad Sci. 2016 Jun; 1373(1): 96–113. doi: 10.1111/nyas.13171 PMCID: PMC5866730 NIHMSID: NIHMS950519 PMID: 27398642

232 Vago R, Zeidan F. The brain on silent: mind wandering, mindful awareness, and states of mental tranquility. Published in final edited form as: Ann N Y Acad Sci. 2016 Jun; 1373(1): 96–113. doi: 10.1111/nyas.13171 PMCID: PMC5866730 NIHMSID: NIHMS950519 PMID: 27398642

233 Koch C. Neuroscience: A quest for consciousness. *Nature* volume 488, pages29–30 (2012)

234 Kandel E. The Age of Insight: The Quest to Understand the Unconscious in Art, Mind, and Brain, from Vienna 1900 to the Present. Random House. 2012.03.2 ISBN 1400058711. https://neurosciencenews.com

235 Whitford P. Christial Quietude. eExpository Times. First Published July 1, 1894 Research Article. https://doi/org.1177/001452469400501005

236 Whitford P. Christial Quietude. eExpository Times. First Published July 1, 1894 Research Article. https://doi/org.1177/001452469400501005

237 https://www.google.com/search?q=fMRI+in+the+brain+in+quititude&tbm=isch&source=univ&client=firefox-b-1-d&sa=X-

&ved=2ahUKEwiax7mRz6LlAhUyTt8KHaBqD2MQsAR-6BAgFEAE&biw=1320&bih=686

238 https://www.google.com/search?q=fMRI+in+the+brain+in-silent+prayer&tbm=isch&source=univ&client=fire-fox-b-1-d&sa=X&ved=2ahUKEwjR4t-01KLlAhUyh-AKHZ5U DXIQsAR6BAgGEAE&biw=1320&bih=686

239 https://www.google.com/search?q=fMRI+in+the+brain+in-silent+prayer&tbm=isch&source=univ&client=fire-fox-b-1-d&sa=X&ved=2ahUKEwjR4t-01KLlAhUyh-AKHZ5U DXIQsAR6BAgGEAE&biw=1320&bih=686

240 https://en.wikipedia.org/wiki/Quality_of_life

241 Singer, P. (2011). "The Big Question: Quality of Life: What Does It Mean? How Should We Measure It?". World Policy Journal. 28 (2): 3–6. doi:10.1177/0740277511415049. PMID 22165429

242 https://en.wiktionary.org/wiki/rejoice#English

243 Williams PB. Searches related to neuroscience of remembering the feeling of joy the functional neuroanatomy of pleasure and happiness.http://truehomewithin.net/Dharma_essays_files/essay_joy10_brain_on_happiness2.pdf

244 Kinglebrach ML, Berridge KO. The Neuroscience of Happiness and Pleasure. Soc Res (New York). Author manuscript; available in PMC 2011 Jul 1. Published in final edited form as: Soc Res (New York). 2010 SUMMER; 77(2): 659–678. PMCID: PMC3008658 NIHMSID: NIHMS257673 PMID: 22068342

245 Callard F, Margolis DS. The Subject at Rest: Novel conceptualizations of self and brain from cognitive neuroscience's study of the 'resting state'. a nature conference. November 6=8, 2019, Xi'an, China. ttps://link.springer.com/article/10.1057/sub.2011.11#Tab1

246 https://nccih.nih.gov/health/stress/relaxation.htm

247 Zargarzadeh M. Shirazi M. The effect of progressive muscle relaxation method on test anxiety in nursing students Iran J Nurs Midwifery Res. 2014 Nov-Dec; 19(6): 607–612. PMCID: PMC4280725 PMID: 25558258

248 https://en.wikipedia.org/wiki/Progressive_muscle_relaxation

249 MS, Blum CM, Hood CJ. Progressive Muscle Relaxation. Journal of Human Behavior in the Social Environment. Volume 13, 2006—Issue 3 Pages 51-66. Published

250 Gessel GH. Edmund Jacobson, M.D., Ph.D.: The Founder of Scientific Relaxation. Adapted from International Journal of Psychosomatics Vol. 36(1-4), 1989. Vol. 36(1-4), 1989. https://www.ncbi.nlm.nih.gov/pmc/articles/PMC4280725/#.

251 Wantess SB. The Role of Psychological Safety in Human Development. Journal Research in Human Development. Volume 13, 2016-Issue 1: Role of Psychological Safety in Human Development. Pages 6-14. Published online: 01 March 2016. Journal Research in Human Development. Volume 13, 2016 - Issue 1: Role of Psychological Safety in Human Development. Journal Research in Human Development. Volume 13, 2016— Issue 1: Role of Psychological Safety in Human Development. https://doi.org/10.1080/15427609.2016.1141283

252 D'Argenmbeau A, Feyeers D, Majerus S, Collette F, Van Der Linden M, Maquet P Salmon E. Self-reflection across time: cortical midline structures differentiate between present and past selves. Soc Cogn Affect Neurosci. 2008 Sep; 3(3): 244–252. Published online 2008 Aug 23. doi: 10.1093/scan/nsn020 PMCID: PMC2566769 PMID: 19015116

253 Murphy T. Journal, *NeuroQuantology* (Vol 8, No 4 (2010) The Role of Religious and Mystic Experiences in Human Evolution: A Corollary Hypothesis for Neurotheology Vol 8, N0 4. 92010)

254 https://en.wikipedia.org/wiki/Neuroscience_of_religion

255 Dimitropoulos S. How Does Neuroscience Explain Spiritual and Religious Experiences? Meditation and Mindfulness for the Western Mind: Fact or Fiction? Aug 18 017. https://medium.com/s/spirits-in-your-brain/how-does-neuroscience-explain-spiritual-and-religious-experiences-3ef8c2f50339

256 Grecussi A, Theunick A, Frederickson J Job R. Mechanism of social emotion regulation: From neuroscience to psychotherapy. Emotion Regulation: Processes, Cognition Effects and Social and Social Consequences Edition: first, Editors Nova

publishers. March_2015._https://www.researchgate.net/publication/271956160. Mechanisms_of_social_emotion_regulat

257  Grecussi A, Theunick A, Frederickson J Job R. Mechanism of social emotion regulation: From neuroscience to psychotherapy. Emotion Regulation: Processes, Cognition Effects and Social and Social Consequences Edition: first, Editors Nova publishers. March_2015. https:// www.researchgate.net/publication/271956160. Mechanisms_of_social_emotion_regulat

258  Fosha D, Siegle DJ, Soloman M. The Healing Power of Emotions: Affective Neuroscience, Development & Clinical Practice, pages 1-28. 2009. https://books.google.com

259  Pepper E, Harvey R, Hamiel D. NeuroRegulation. Transforming Thoughts with Postural Awareness to Increase Therapeutic and Teaching Efficacy. http://www.isnr.org153. www.neuroregulation.org. Vol. 6(3):153–1602019doi:10.15540/nr.6.3.153

260  https://en.wiktionary.org/wiki/thankfulness#English

261  https://en.wikipedia.org/wiki/Gratitude

262  http://www.thewisdompost.com/law-of-attraction/gratitude/what-is-the-difference-between-gratitude-and-thankfulness/1163

263  https://en.wiktionary.org/wiki/tenderness

264  ps://press.vatican.va/content/salastampa/en/ bollettino/ pubblico/2018/09/13/180913

265  https://en.wikipedia.org/wiki/Truthfulnesshttps:// en.wikipedia.org/wiki/Truthfulness

266  http://engeneic.com/m6b5ecoo/honesty-and-truthfulness-definition.html

267  https://en.wiktionary.org/wiki/thoughtfulness#English

268  https://www.poetrysoup.com/dictionary/thoughtfulness

269  https://en.wiktionary.org/wiki/understanding

270  https://en.wikipedia.org/wiki/Understanding

271  D'Drgembeau A, Feyers D, Majerus D, Collette F, Van Der Linden M. Self-reflection across time: cortical midline structures differentiate between present and past selves. Soc Cogn Affect Neurosci. 2008 Sep; 3(3): 244–252. Published online 2008 Aug

23. doi: 10.1093/scan/nsn020 PMCID: PMC2566769PMID: 19015116

272 https:// en.wikipedia.org/wiki/Creative_visualization#Stages

273 Kurniawan IT, Guttart-Masip M, Dayan P, Dolan RJ. Effort and Valuation in the Brain: The Effects of Anticipation and Execution. Journal of Neuroscience 3 April 2013, 33 (14) 6160-6169; DOI: https://doi.org/10.1523/JNEUROSCI.4777-12.2013

274 Flammer A. Self-efficacy. International Encyclopedia of the Social & Behavioral Sciences. 2001, Pages 13812-13815. https://doi.org/10.1016/B0-08-043076-7/01726-5

275 https://en.wikipedia.org/wiki/Well-being

276 Meeks TW, Jest DV. Neurobiology of Wisdom A Literature Overview. JAMA Psychiatric. ArchGen Psychiatry. 2009;66(4):355-365. doi: 10:1001/arcgenpychology.2009.8

277 https://en.wiktionary.org/wiki/wholesome

278 Dimitropoulos S. How Does Neuroscience Explain Spiritual and Religious Experiences? Meditation and Mindfulness for the Western Mind: Fact or Fiction? Aug 18 017. https:// medium. com/s/spirits-in-your-brain/how-does-neuroscience-explain-spiritual-and- religious-experiences- 3ef8c2f50339

279 Divine Action Topic: Neuroscience and the Person. https:// counterbalance.org.clins-vo/ neuro-frame.html

280 https://www.uuberks.org/sandras-study/what-does-it-mean-live-life-yearning

281 https://www.psychologytoday.com/us/blog/is-it-beautiful/2019 03/spiritual-yearning

282 Klein NA, Goldstein RZ, Tomasi D, Zhang L, Jones SP, Telang F, Wang G-J, Fowler JS, Volkow ND. What is in a Word? *No* versus *Yes* Differentially Engage the Lateral Orbitofrontal Cortex. Emotion. Author manuscript; available in PMC 2008 Jul 7. Published in final edited form as: Emotion. 2007 Aug; 7(3): 649–659. doi: 10.1037/1528- 3542.7.3.649 PMCID: PMC2443710 NIHMSID: NIHMS53710 PMID: 17683220

283 https://positivepsychology.com/zest/

284 https://english.stackexchange.com/questions/490220/ zeal-vs-zest-am-i-using-them- correctly

285 Duckworth AL, Eichstaedt JC, Ungar L. The Mechanics of Human Achievement. Soc Personal Psychol Compass. Author manuscript; available in PMC 2016 Jul 1. Published in final edited form as: Soc Personal Psychol Compass. 2015 Jul; 9(7): 359–369. Published online 2015 Jul 2. doi:10.1111/spc3.12178 PMCID: PMC4520322 NIHMSID: NIHMS688901 PMID: 26236393

286 Hare TA, Camerer CF, Rangel A. Self-Control in Decision-Making Involves Modulation of the vm PFC Valuation System. *Science* 01 May 2009: Vol. 324, Issue 5927, pp. 646-648. DOI:10.1126/science.1168450

287 *******Gilbert P. Psychotherapy for the 21st century: An integrative, evolutionary, contextual, biopsychosocial approach. Psychol Psychother. 2019 Jun; 92(2): 164–189. Published online 2019 Apr 1.doi: 10.1111/papt.12226 PMCID: PMC6593829 PMID: 30932302

288 https://en.wikipedia.org/wiki/Autosuggestion

289 Promises. Stanford Encyclopedia on Philosophy. First published Fri Oct 10, 2008; substantive revision Tue Mar 4, 2014

290 Habib, A, 2009, "Promises to the Self", *Canadian Journal of Philosophy*, 39(4): 537-557.

291 Rosati CS. The Importance of Self-Promises Chapter 5 in Promises and Agreements: Philosophical Essays ed. Hanoch Sheinman. Print publication date: 2011Print ISBN-13: 9780195377958. Published to Oxford Scholarship Online: May 2011 DOI: 10.1093/acprof:oso/ 9780195377958.001.0001

292 Kurji AH. Promises to the Self, Chapter 3.1. An Update Semantics for Promises and Other Obligations-Creating Speech Acts, A promising Start. MSc Thesis written by Aadil Hanif Kurji (born October 11th, 1983 in Calgary, Canada) under the supervision of Prof Dr Frank Voltman and submitted to the Board of Examiners in partial fulfillment of the requirements for the degree of MSc in Logic at the Universiteit van Amsterdam. Date if the public defense October 9, 2012.https://www.academia.edu/3426654/An Update Semantics for Promises and Other Obligations Creating Speech Acts

# ABOUT THE AUTHOR

Dr. Ron Kelley, graduate of the University of Louisville School of Medicine in 1968, is a practicing psychiatrist who completed his residency at Walter Reed General Hospital and Medical Center in 1972. He was chief of psychiatry at Ft. Campbell, Kentucky, in 1972–1973, after which he was a Second Infantry Division psychiatrist in the Republic of Korea from 1973 to 1974. He is a past president of the Kentucky Psychiatric Association and past chief of the medical staff of Lourdes Hospital in Paducah, Kentucky; a Distinguished Life Fellow of the American Psychiatric Association; an assistant professor of clinical psychiatry of the University of Kentucky Medical School, and has been in private practice since 1975.

Dr. Kelley first began to develop the beginning of the ABCs of Healing Feelings over three decades ago. Realizing, as others before, that his patients with undeveloped emotional ego skills were not fully benefitting from psychotherapy, Dr. Kelley created a collection of practical mind management tools known as "The Kelley ABCs of Healing Feelings."

Ron Kelley lives in Paducah, Kentucky, with beautiful Molly, "The love of his life."